Teaching and Personality

for Elizabeth

Teaching and Personality

DAVID FONTANA

Basil Blackwell

© David Fontana 1977

First published 1977 by Open Books Publishing Ltd

Second edition published 1986

Basil Blackwell Ltd
108 Cowley Road, Oxford OX4 1JF, UK

Basil Blackwell Inc.
432 Park Avenue South, Suite 1503,
New York, NY 10016, USA

British Library Cataloguing in Publication Data

Fontana, David
 Teaching and Personality — Rev. ed.
 1. School children — Psychology
 2. Personality
 I. Title II. Fontana, David. Personality
 and education
 370.15'3 BF713

ISBN 0-631-14913-9
ISBN 0-631-14914-7 PBK

Library of Congress Cataloging in Publication Data

Fontana, David.
 Teaching and personality.
 Rev., updated ed. of: Personality and education, c1977.
 Bibliography: p.
 Includes indexes.
 1. Educational psychology. 2. Personality. 3. Child
development. I. Fontana, David, Personality and
education. II. Title.
LB1051.F555 1986 370.15'3 85-28685
ISBN 0-631-14913-9
ISBN 0-631-14914-7 (pbk.)

Phototypeset by Dobbie Typesetting Service, Plymouth, Devon
Printed in Great Britain by Billing & Sons Ltd, Worcester

Contents

Preface to the New Edition

In the years since the first edition of this book (then entitled *Personality and Education*), there have been a number of exciting developments in the study of personality. Some well-established viewpoints, such as Freudian theory, have come under forceful attack, while certain new approaches, for example George Kelly's personal construct theory, have steadily gained in popularity. Yet other work, such as investigations into cognitive style, while remaining potentially valuable, has appeared to mark time, increasingly in need of new research initiatives.

Perhaps the most important development, however, has been in the state-based approach to personality, that is the approach which sees personality as a fluid, ever-changing process rather than as a set of relatively enduring traits. Much of the current debate in personality studies lies between the respective advocates of state-based and trait-based theories, and this debate is likely to remain an intense and interesting one. In view of the importance and implications of this controversy and of the many other new developments in personality study, it has been necessary to incorporate much fresh material in this second edition. New chapters have been added on the state-based approach and on the vital issue of teacher personality (including teacher stress). At the same time, the opportunity has been taken to recast existing chapters, eliminating topics that were attracting attention when the first edition was written but which have since dropped out of the limelight, and incorporating new ideas that are now becoming prominent. References and reports of research findings have been fully updated, and new terminology introduced where appropriate.

Nevertheless, the aim of the book remains the same. It is to give teachers and all those interested in education an introduction to the whole field of personality, emphasising throughout the practical lessons that can be drawn for use in the classroom. The approach is intended to be a balanced one, presenting all relevant shades of opinion rather than focusing exclusively on any one set of views. Where possible, the intention is to show that, far from conflicting with one another, each of these shades of opinion has its own particular contribution to make to the practical tasks of the teacher. Each advances in its own way our understanding of children, and of the methods by which teachers can assist children towards satisfactory personality development. Throughout the book the emphasis is not upon personality theories and models for their own sake, but upon these theories and models as a way of improving the professional skills and confidence of the teacher.

Grateful thanks are due to Patrick Taylor of Open Books, who published the first edition of this book, for his support and encouragement.

David Fontana

Introduction

The aim of this book is to discuss those psychological insights into personality that are of most relevance to education. At the end of it, the reader should know something of the origins and development of personality, something of those theories of personality that crop up most frequently in educational discussion, something of the most popular devices for measuring personality, and should understand the implications of these topics for the work of the teacher. Because it is an introductory text, the purpose will be to draw the reader's attention to what is important, rather than to go into things in great detail. Personality is such a vast field within psychology that we cannot hope to do more.

Perhaps this is as good a place as any to make one important reservation. That is, that, although the psychologist has spent a great deal of time and effort researching into personality over the last half-century or so, he is still very far from knowing the whole truth about it. Psychologists like to construct theories and to measure things. I hope I shall say enough in this book to show that these activities tell us sufficient about personality to influence profoundly the way in which the teacher thinks about children. But theories and measurements can only take us so far. I may, for example, construct a theory on the meaning of happiness, devise a test to measure its presence in people, and then find that two children get identical scores on my test. But this doesn't mean that their relative degrees of happiness can really be reduced to equal marks on a paper and pencil test. Even if my test is a good one, it still doesn't tell me whether the two children will be made equally happy by the same events. Nor does it tell me how happiness *feels* to the children, the extent to which in each case it can stand up to the blows of fate, the extent to which it will change with time, and so on. Teachers, perhaps more than anyone else, know that children are unique. The only way to know a child is, obviously enough, to get to know him. Psychology books are aids towards, and not substitutes for, this process of getting to know.

What is personality?

The teacher is interested in children's personalities for two reasons. First, because of a concern with how children develop as people – that is, with how they relate to others and to themselves, how they develop goals and ambitions in life, how they acquire codes of conduct and styles of behaviour, and how they adjust to the inevitable problems and challenges that are part of being human. And, secondly, because of a concern with the way in which these factors influence a child's academic achievement, since we know that this achievement is dependent not just upon such things as intelligence but upon the whole range of personal functioning that the child brings to bear upon the learning task.

Our first problem arises, however, when we come to define personality. Personality is one of those tantalising terms' that seems to retreat the further from us the more we try to grasp it. We all think we know what the word means, but the effort of expressing this meaning in any generally acceptable form is often beyond us. Psychologists are no exception to this. As long ago as 1937, Allport listed no fewer than fifty attempts by psychologists at definition, and commented that some of them were so all-embracing that they included practically everything that interests the psychologist about people – for instance, 'personality is the entire mental organisation of a human being at any stage in his development'.

More recently, psychologists have tried to be more precise by taking personality to include only such things as sentiments, attitudes, complexes and unconscious mechanisms, interests and ideals (Vernon 1975), and have excluded from it cognitive and physical attributes such as intelligence and motor skills. The term 'affective' is sometimes used to distinguish personality variables from cognitive or physical ones, but strictly speaking this term relates only to those aspects of personality which have to do directly with the emotions.

Having made this distinction between personality and cognitive and physical variables, we now have to admit that the three influence each other so closely that the layman may feel that this distinction has more to do with the psychologist's convenience than with anything else. Psychology is such a vast subject that it has to be parcelled up into more manageable units, even if the parcelling is somewhat arbitrary. But separating personality in this way from cognitive factors helps us at least to focus attention upon man as a creature of feelings and moods as well as a creature of intelligence. It helps us to emphasise that he is a social creature, with characteristic ways of reacting to others and towards himself, a creature of beliefs, aspirations and dreams, a creature ruled, as the ancients had it, by the heart as well as by the head.

One of the most satisfactory recent attempts to define personality is that in Eysenck, Arnold and Meili (1975):

Personality is the relatively stable organisation of a person's motivational dispositions, arising from the interaction between biological drives and the social and physical environment. The term . . . usually refers chiefly to the affective–conative traits, sentiments, attitudes, complexes and unconscious mechanisms, interests and ideals, which determine man's characteristic or distinctive behaviour and thought.

This definition stresses not only the content of personality, but also that personality is *stable* (i.e. we do not change into fundamentally different people from day to day), that it is *organised* (i.e. that its attributes are interrelated), that it is formed as a result of *interaction* between innate biological mechanisms and the environment, and that it is *distinctive* (i.e. that each personality is unique).

I shall adopt this as my basic definition, but it is necessary to make three further points. First, the psychologist never uses 'personality' in the value-loaded sense often employed by the layman. Popularly, to have or to be full of 'personality' means to be outgoing, lively and interesting, and to be lacking in it implies the opposite. But to the psychologist everyone has personality. The emphasis is upon understanding people, not upon passing social judgements upon them. Secondly, the word 'character' is sometimes used synonymously with 'personality' in ordinary conversation. The former comes from a Greek word meaning 'engraving', while the latter is from a Latin one meaning 'mask'. The former would thus seem to be something deep and fixed (i.e. innate), and the latter something superficial (i.e. acquired). Paradoxically, some psychologists take the former to mean acquired attributes and the latter to mean innate. This is confusing, and I shall in consequence avoid the term 'character', and stick to 'personality', taking it to refer to both innate and acquired factors.

The third point is that, since the aim of this book is to draw attention to all those areas of personality of practical relevance to the teacher, we shall have to cover a great deal of ground. Inevitably, in a subject as rich and complex as human psychology, this will mean introducing the reader sometimes to the work of psychologists who appear to stand in disagreement with each other. Nevertheless, much of this disagreement is more apparent than real. It is rather as if the psychologists are simply looking at the same scenery from different vantage points. If we want to build up an accurate description of the scenery, we therefore have to fit their various descriptions together.

One final observation. There is no satisfactory way of avoiding the pronouns 'he' and 'she' in a book of this kind. Since most of what I have to say applies equally to boy and girl pupils and to male and female teachers this raises problems. The continual use of 'he or she' is likely to prove irksome to the reader, while hybrid terms such as s/he are too impersonal. Accordingly I have used the convention of 'she' for the teacher and 'he' for the pupil, but it could just as readily have been the other way around. Where there are specific differences between the sexes to be taken into account, this will be made clear.

1

Personality Determinants

The teacher has an obvious interest in the determinants of personality. Only by knowing where personality comes from can he or she decide the extent to which the personalities of children are fixed by what happens outside school, and the extent to which they can be altered by what happens inside it. If we look back to the definition of personality quoted on page 3, we can see that we have already committed ourselves to the view that personality is the result of interaction between inherited and environmental factors, and we need now to look at the evidence for this view, taking heredity first.

The influence of heredity upon personality

Common observation has always led people to believe that we each inherit something of our personalities. We say that Mary has her father's calmness, that John has his mother's love of music, that Peter has his grandfather's determination. We describe people as born optimists or pessimists, as born teachers or nurses or comedians. But common observation could be wrong in ascribing these things to inheritance. They could just as easily be acquired through the close contacts which children have with their parents during the early formative years of their lives. Mary may have learnt the value of calmness from the calm way in which her father treated her; Peter may be determined because his mother admired this quality in her own father and sought to encourage it in her son; and the 'born' comedian may simply have found that making people laugh was the one sure way to get their attention when he was a boy.

The difficulty of separating the relative influence of heredity and environment in any area of psychological development is considerable (witness, for example, the continuing debate over the origins of measured intelligence). From the moment of birth onwards – indeed, from the moment of conception, since the inter-uterine environment itself is important – heredity and environment interact with each other in a highly complex way. Many of the experiments which might help the psychologist to distinguish their relative importance, such as keeping the individual in a strictly controlled environment from birth, and denying him certain kinds of potentially valuable stimuli, are ethically unacceptable (which is one of the reasons why the psychologist so often falls back upon experiments with animals), and, more often than we care to admit, the limited experiments that we can carry out produce conflicting results.

Some of our strongest evidence for the role of heredity in personality comes, therefore, not from psychology but from our knowledge of the biological mechanisms of inheritance. A good, simple account of these mechanisms is given in Mussen, Conger and Kagan (1984), and all that we need to say here is that at conception each normal child, with the exception of identical twins, receives a unique complement of forty-six chromosomes, twenty-three from each parent, and that these chromosomes contain the genes responsible for the transmission of attributes from the parents to the child. Our biological knowledge is not yet sufficiently advanced to tell us which precise genes transmit which precise attributes, but it is known that physical characteristics such as potential height and weight, colour of hair and eyes, size of feet and hands, and so on, are all in some way genetically determined. Importantly for our purposes, there is also evidence that genes play a part in determining individual differences in behaviour.

Much of this evidence comes from studying people who have inherited chromosomal, and therefore genetic, abnormalities of one kind or another. For example, Down's syndrome (mongolism), which accounts for some 15 per cent of patients in institutions for the subnormal, is present in individuals who have inherited an extra chromosome. Turner's syndrome, which produces abnormal shortness together with diminished mental ability, attention span and memory, shows itself in girls who lack the normal complement of sex chromosomes. And choreoathetosis, a disease in which children exhibit spastic symptoms, self-mutilation, and extreme aggression, seems likely also to be owing to an inherited defect. Finally, Price and Whatmore (1967) produced evidence, since questioned, suggesting that among men who have inherited an extra male sex chromosome, there is a greater than normal incidence of instability and severe personality disorder, of early conviction for delinquent offences, and of eventual committal to institutions for the mentally subnormal and violent offender.

Of course, the fact that chromosomes are implicated in certain kinds of abnormal behaviour does not mean that they are necessarily also implicated in normal behaviour, but it does provide useful pointers in that direction. Following a similar clue, we can also look at those children who inherit identical chromosomes at conception, i.e. identical twins, and see if their personalities are any more alike than are those of fraternal twins. Identical, or monozygotic, twins (MZ for short) are formed from a single ovum and a single sperm which, in the course of normal cell division, split completely into two separate embryos, while fraternal, or dizygotic (DZ), twins are formed from two separate ovums and two separate sperms and are no more alike genetically than are any other siblings.

Assuming that the twins in each MZ and DZ pair are brought up in similar environments, if MZ twins do prove to resemble each other more closely than do DZ twins, we should be justified in seeing this as evidence for heredity. Research, in fact, shows the existence of just such a resemblance. Eysenck (e.g. 1983) reports evidence for closer similarities between MZ than between DZ twins on a range of personality measures (see chapter 5 below). In a comparison between ordinary siblings as well as twins, Cattell and his colleagues (see Scheinfeld 1973) concluded that heredity weighs more heavily than environment on such personality traits as warm-heartedness and sociability.

So far so good, but the problem has further complications. MZ and DZ twins may *not* enjoy similar environments. MZ twins, who are always of the same sex, and who resemble each other closely physically, are often treated consciously much more alike by their parents than are DZ twins. They are also treated more alike by other adults and by school friends, many of whom cannot tell them apart. The only way to avoid this problem is to look at instances where MZ and DZ twins have been separated at birth and each brought up in a different home. An early study by Newman, Freeman and Holzinger (1937) concluded that even here MZ twins resembled each other on personality measures more closely than did DZ twins, while Shields (1962) found that, on Eysenck's measures of extroversion and neuroticism, the resemblance between MZ twins was so much greater than that between DZs that even MZ twins reared apart were more alike than DZs reared together.

Fortunately from a humane point of view, but unfortunately from that of the researcher, instances of MZ twins reared apart are rare, and we cannot regard the samples in the above studies as large enough to put the matter beyond dispute. Taking the whole range of twin-studies however, and applying statistical techniques, Eysenck has attempted to answer the question of *how much* of the measurable personality differences between people is owing to heredity and how much to environment, and has concluded that, for his own measures of neuroticism and extroversion at least, 65 per cent may be owing to heredity (Eysenck 1978).

More evidence for the role of heredity comes from studies which seek a relationship between physique and personality. We know that the former is genetically strongly influenced, and, if it can be established that certain kinds of physique usually go with certain kinds of personality, this might argue a genetic basis for the latter as well. If we go back to common observation again, we find that people have long claimed the physique-personality relationship to exist. The ancient Greeks, who studied man almost as keenly as the modern psychologist, held that people resembled in temperament those animals they most closely resembled in appearance (perhaps there are still echoes of this when we describe people as sheepish, or bovine, or wolfish, or owl-like), while Shakespeare's reference to men with a 'lean and hungry look' as being more thoughtful and dangerous than those who are fat has passed into popular speech, along with many other examples of his acute observations about his fellow men.

Whether the modern psychologist can improve very much upon the Greeks and Shakespeare in this field is open to question, but extensive work in it was carried out over a quarter-century and more by the American William Sheldon. On the basis of studies with large samples of people, Sheldon postulated the existence of three basic types of body-build, the *endomorph*, who is round and fat, the *mesomorph*, who is hard and muscular, and the *ectomorph*, who is lean and delicate. Personality tests with the same samples revealed that each body build seems to have a corresponding set of personality characteristics:

the endomorph is tolerant, complacent, sociable, easy-going, affectionate and dependent;
the mesomorph is aggressive, tough-minded, competitive, energetic and dominating;
the ectomorph is restrained, withdrawn, intellectual and anxious.

Nobody belongs exclusively to only one of these types. We each of us have elements of all three in us, and in measuring a person's physique Sheldon assigned a score from 1 to 7 on each of them (known as his *somatotype*). Thus an extreme endomorph might score 7-1-1, an extreme mesormorph 1-7-1, and an extreme ecto-morph 1-1-7. In practice, such extremes are rare, though in most people one of these scores will predominate over the other two.

The work of Sheldon and his associates indicated that these three physical types are found in both sexes, that the somatotype can be assessed reliably from age six onwards, and that it remains relatively constant throughout life (e.g. Sheldon 1954). True, many people put on weight or get more muscular as they grow older, but these gains can be fairly accurately predicted from a knowledge of the individual's somatotype at the end of adolescence (Parnell 1958).

Unfortunately, Sheldon's findings were not fully confirmed by other investigators. Some claimed not to find the same three physical types, while others doubted the relationship between them and personality. However, further work by Sheldon (Sheldon et al. 1969) uncovered additional corroborative evidence, and his assertions seem, partially at least, to be well founded. It would be nice to leave it at that, and to move on to the next point, but once again it is necessary to admit to a snag. Sheldon's findings might have nothing to do with heredity at all. Muscular people may be more aggressive and competitive than fat or thin people simply because life has taught them that with their physical strength aggression and competitiveness pay off, while thin people, who find the reverse to be true, retire discreetly to their books. Alternatively, though less likely, child-rearing practices may be responsible, with the fat person developing both his broad waistline and his love of comfort in response to an over-indulgent mother.

The most reasonable conclusion is probably that both heredity and environment lie behind the physique–personality relation-ship. From an educational point of view, Sheldon's work attracted particular interest because correlations were found between the somatotype and, respectively, personality disorders and educational achievement. For example, samples of delinquent youths were shown to contain a significantly large percentage of mesomorphs (Glueck and Glueck 1956), while samples of good honours-degree holders were found to show a significant tendency towards ectomorphy (Parnell 1958). Eysenck has suggested in the past that, if the somatotype does give us an insight into inherited personality characteristics, it would be of use to take a simplified measurement of it, based upon height–weight ratio and chest girth, as a part of the routine school medical examination. This would give us a clue, from an early age, to the trend of a child's future personality development, and would help us to avoid making demands which the child is temperamentally unable to fulfil (though it might have the corresponding disadvantage of serving as a self-fulfilling prophecy). Unfortunately little new research into Sheldon's work has been carried out in recent years, which means we are still unable to draw very firm conclusions from it, though Wells (1983) reaffirms its importance.

Another approach to the relationship between heredity and personality is the longitudinal study. Researchers look for evidence of temperamental differences between babies in the early days of life, when environment has had little chance to exert any influence, and then follow them through into later life to see if these differences are still apparent. One of the best longitudinal studies is that of the American researchers Thomas, Chess and Birch (1970). Taking a sample of 141 children, initially aged eight to twelve weeks, the researchers obtained ratings for them from parents and social workers on such items of behaviour as activity levels, regularity of bodily functions (feeding, sleeping, etc.), adaptability, sensitivity to stimuli, and disposition (cheerful, cranky, etc.). Results showed that 65 per cent of the children could be assigned unequivocally to one of three groups:

the easy group, characterised by regular body-functioning, adaptability, a positive approach to new people and objects, low reaction levels, and cheerfulness of mood (40 per cent of sample);

the difficult group, characterised by irregular body-functioning, low adaptability, a negative approach to new people and objects, overreaction to stimuli, and negativity of mood (10 per cent of sample);

the slow-to-warm-up group, characterised by low activity levels, low adaptability, some withdrawal in the face of new people and objects, mild reaction levels, and slight negativity of mood (15 per cent of sample).

The sample has now been followed through childhood and into adolescence, and membership of the groups has remained markedly constant. Not surprisingly, the easy group have presented fewer problems. When they started school, they proved readily adaptable, joined in activities, and learnt rules quickly. Only 18 per cent of them have developed behaviour problems, as opposed to 70 per cent of the difficult group.

Obviously environmental factors will by now have played some part in heightening or diminishing these temperamental characteristics, but that environment is not the *cause* of them is evidenced by the fact that the researchers have found parental behaviour styles to be evenly distributed across the three groups of children. Where these styles have been an important variable, however, is in the success with which each group of children has come to terms with these characteristics. Easy children have flourished under most parental styles (this would probably not have been so had there been any really bad parents in the sample), but the difficult children have become increasingly awkward and negative if reared by inconsistent, impatient or excessively punitive parents. Difficult children, it seems, need extra skilful, objective and painstaking handling. And the same appears to be true of those who are slow to warm-up. These children have shown a particular need for encouragement and parental support. Without it, or in the face of abrupt precipitation into new experiences, they have tended to withdraw even further into themselves. The key to success with them seems to have been to present them with plenty of new and interesting stimuli, but to allow them to tackle these stimuli at their own pace, providing plentiful praise and guidance, and encouraging them not to give up in the face of difficulties.

Thomas, Chess and Birch's findings that early temperamental characteristics provide a reliable guide to future personality development allow us to agree with Allport (1961) that what we seem to inherit is the raw material of our personality ('temperament' is as good a word for this raw material as any). Environment, in ways which we shall be examining in the next section, then moulds this raw material into its mature form. The importance of this to the teacher is emphasised by Thomas, Chess and Birch themselves. They point out that temperament affects a great deal of what a child does in school, from the way in which he relates to his teacher and other children, to the way in which he tackles the learning task. A child with high activity levels is likely to become frustrated and fidgety if made to sit still for too long; a child with a short attention span may respond well only in an environment with plenty of variety; a slow-to-warm-up child may need repeated and patient exposure to a learning task before he becomes confident enough to be able to tackle it; and a child with a negative and whimsical disposition may become worse if his own mood is matched with a similar one, or with anger and a battle of wills, by the teacher.

Of great relevance to the more general debate on teaching-methods, Thomas, Chess and Birch found that an overpermissive atmosphere was particularly unsuitable for the difficult child, who did better on clear and patient guidance from the teacher in a more formal structured classroom. It seems probable that the slow-to-warm-up child might well also flourish more in such a classroom, and might run the risk of passing unnoticed in a particularly open and active environment.

This does not mean that I am entering a plea for formal teaching-methods. Far from it. But it does mean that there is no single set of methods which is of optimum benefit for all children. An active, outgoing, sociable child may do much better in an informal than in a formal setting, and the opposite may be true of a more withdrawn or hesitant child. So, whatever methods the teacher uses, she must be alert to children as individuals, which is very difficult in a large class, but which is an essential aspect of the teacher's role. We shall be returning to this point at greater length in the next section.

Environment

Having examined the importance of heredity in personality, we now turn to environment. The obvious place to start is in the home, where the child spends all his early years and a large proportion of his later ones. Within the home, most research interest has focused on the mother–child relationship. It is the mother who normally supplies the child with most of his stimuli. It is she who feeds him, cares for him, plays with him, and often decides what behaviour is acceptable and what unacceptable from him. It is she who provides him with love, and with an audience for much of his early activity. It is she who takes him to school when he grows older, and she to whom he tells his problems. This is not to minimise the role of the father, nor is it to ignore the fact that some of the mother's role is often shared with other adults, and that in some homes the roles of mother and father are reversed. We shall have more to say about this later. Here it suffices to stress that, for the majority of children, the mother provides the main human link with the outside world in the early years of life.

One way of assessing the importance of this link in the formation of the child's personality is to look at those instances where the child is deprived of adequate care through maternal death or neglect. Unfortunately the evidence here is not as clearcut as one would like, partly because so many other factors (the quality of substitute care, the reasons for the child's separation from parents, life-events following the separation, socioeconomic factors, age and sex of the child – to name only a few) enter into the equation. Earlier studies such as those of Goldfarb (1955) and Trasler (1960) showed that children placed for adoption early in life were much more likely to show satisfactory subsequent personality development than those who remained in institutions for much of their first three years and were only placed for adoption later on. On the other hand Clarke and Clarke (1976) point to evidence that, even when children suffer severe deprivation in the early years, their later development may still be satisfactory given appropriate subsequent support. Perhaps these two somewhat opposing views are best reconciled by Rutter (1976), who concludes that, although single brief instances of parental separation or neglect rarely have long-term effects upon the child, recurrent instances may well have, particularly if other forms of disadvantage are also present.

We must stress in addition that children who suffer deprivation in the early years of life all too frequently do *not* have appropriate support to compensate them in the years that follow. Thus, whether or not we regard the first few years of life as any more crucial for personality development than the years that follow, research evidence leaves us in little doubt that children who are denied appropriate care by a mother or mother-substitute for significant periods of childhood run grave risks of long-term personality damage.

The exact nature of this damage may vary from child to child, but it appears to be much more marked in instances where ill treatment or domestic strife are present and in instances of parental death or prolonged absence. As shown by Rutter (1976), for example, children from homes in which there is both a high degree of parental discord and a low level of warmth in the parent–child relationship show a much greater incidence of disturbed and antisocial behaviour and of attendance at psychiatric clinics than do children from more fortunate homes. It seems that children require warmth and affection and a reasonably stable and secure home life if they are to stand the best chance of developing into the kind of mature personalities we discuss in chapter 2. Even where parental care appears on the surface to be adequate, but where there is in fact a generally cold, strict and censorious attitude on the part of parents, there is likely to be a greater than usual level of feeding-problems, overdependency, poor socialisation and fearfulness amongst children.

Something of the more extreme effects that bad or absent parental care can have upon the young come from experiments with animals and in particular from the work a few years ago of Harold Harlow at the University of Wisconsin. Animal studies will be referred to in this book only rarely, but Harlow's experiments seem to have such obvious potential relevance that they are worth looking at in a little detail.

What Harlow did was to raise several generations of rhesus monkeys under conditions of maternal deprivation and study the results. Monkeys raised in social isolation and with only a simple wire model equipped with a feeding-bottle as a surrogate mother fared worst, showing every sign from infancy onwards of emotional disturbance and withdrawal. They spent most of their time in the corner of their cages, rocking quietly to themselves and cowering in terror if a frightening stimulus was near. They fed at the wire mother-surrogate, but spent little time with her otherwise. When taken outside their cages they showed no confidence in exploring their environment, and indeed manifested all the symptoms of terror and withdrawal that we classify as autism when present in human children.

Monkeys reared with mock-up mother-substitutes covered in a soft terry towelling material fared rather better. They appeared to enjoy the tactile contact of the towelling material, spent much of their time clinging to it in apparent contentment, and using it as a secure base from which to explore any novel stimuli introduced into their cages. At first Harlow concluded that psychological development appeared to proceed normally as long as the infant monkeys were provided with this soft tactile contact, but subsequently (Harlow and Harlow 1962) research showed that by the time they reached the age of three even the towelling-reared monkeys were showing extreme behaviour problems. When eventually allowed to mix with other monkeys they were unable to relate to them satisfactorily either socially or sexually. Those females who eventually became mothers (entirely, it seems, through the commendable persistence and patience of a group of normally reared males) proved themselves to be, in Harlow's words, 'hopeless, helpless and heartless' at the job, either ignoring their offspring altogether or abusing them cruelly.

Although subsequent work by Harlow (Suomi and Harlow 1972) has shown that the stereotyped and bizarre social behaviour of these isolate monkeys can be altered to near normality by placing them with female monkeys three months younger than themselves over a therapeutic period of twenty-six weeks, this hardly lessens the impact of his findings. As we have already indicated, children who are disadvantaged in the early years of life rarely have the opportunity for intensive subsequent remedial care. Early personality damage may indeed be reversible granted the right conditions, but, since these conditions are not readily available to many children, such damage frequently has little to prevent it from becoming long-term. Harlow suggests (Harlow and Harlow 1966) that in monkeys the major damage is done if deprivation takes place for the first six months of life, which is roughly equivalent to the first two or three years of human life. Deprivation for the first sixty days of a monkey's life – equivalent to the first six months or so of human life – may in Harlow's view be reversible, but the longer the period extends beyond this the greater the chance of enduring emotional scars.

Evidence for the importance of environment in personality development does not come only from the home. Numerous studies have shown that children brought up in a so-called middle-class culture tend to have measurable differences in personality from those brought up in an economically underprivileged one. McCandless (1969) has it that middle-class standards and values lead children to espouse hard work, ambition, cleanliness and self-control (particularly in relation to aggression and sex), while working-class standards and values result in children who are more open and uninhibited, and more inclined towards the immediate gratification of needs and impulses. The greater incidence of aggressive, violent and delinquent behaviour amongst working-class children is argued to be directly attributable to the poorer training in social control and to the greater economic and social deprivation and frustration that these children experience (see, for instance, Mussen, Conger and Kagan 1984 for a review of relevant research). Sociological research shows that some working-class sub-groups develop their own sub-cultures which espouse forms of behaviour that are at variance with what is taught at school and by the law of the land. Often these sub-groups lay positive emphasis upon toughness, quick wits, excitement and the desirability of resisting restraint, and, whether he likes it or not, the child grows up believing that such things are the norm until he starts school and comes into conflict with a quite different order of things.

From the point of view of the teacher, the particular importance of the findings quoted in this chapter is that the child who appears awkward or difficult, violent or aggressive, withdrawn or sullen, should not automatically be held to blame. In the chapters on personality and learning-theory, we shall be looking at how far psychologists hold us to be responsible for our own behaviour (and incidentally seeing that there is a fair measure of disagreement amongst them) but for the present the important thing is to stress that a child's personality is not his own wilful creation. Teachers and others who are concerned with the alleged decline in standards of behaviour amongst the young are sometimes prone to blame it upon the influence that psychologists have had upon child-rearing practices. This is unfair. As will be noted throughout the book, the psychologist emphasises the importance of clear and consistent standards in the education of the young, but insists that, before we start trying to 'correct' a child, we first take the trouble to understand why he is as he is. Only then are the methods that we use to change him likely to be well chosen, and the changes beneficial to him as well as to the adults in his life.

2

Personality Development

The first three years of life, during which, as we have seen, the effects of maternal deprivation seem particularly hard to reverse, are an example of what the psychologist calls a *critical period* in the development of the child. A critical period is, in fact, any stage in human or animal development during which the organism is maximally sensitive to the presence of certain kinds of stimuli. Denied these stimuli, behaviour which is regarded as characteristic of the species concerned may not develop, even though there is often a considerable gap in time between the critical period and the age at which the behaviour normally occurs. Thus, deprived of mothering themselves in infancy, Harlow's monkeys grew up with inadequate mothering-skills of their own, and the same may well hold true for humans, as any veteran social worker who has watched the depressing cycle of aggressive and violent mothering-styles pass from one generation to the next will readily attest.

One question that is sometimes asked is, why should children who are shamefully treated by their mothers during the early years of life often show great affection for them, even though they are incapable of showing it to anyone else? One answer is that proposed by Hess (1970): namely, that in these early years children may have a natural tendency to seek proximity to other people, and that whoever happens to be proximate during the critical period becomes the object of an enduring attachment. The point Hess is making is that this attachment is a mechanical one. The child attaches himself to his mother simply because she happens to be there. There is no element of choice in the matter. Such an attachment would have obvious survival value, and may be akin to imprinting in animals, that instinct that prompts some creatures to attach themselves to the first moving object they see during the early hours of life, and to remain attached to it through thick and thin (however embarrassing this may prove to the object concerned, should it happen to be the research psychologist himself).

In the case of humans, it is wiser not to be too specific as to when critical periods occur, but rather to regard the whole of childhood as such a period, with great variation between children as to which particular years of childhood are critical for which particular kinds of development. There may, as we indicated above, even be children who can survive severe maternal deprivation in the first three years or so of life, and yet still appear, on the surface at least, unscarred, but they are probably few in number.

What must be stressed is that what happens to the child during childhood is not really analogous to the rational experiences of the adult, which happen to a physiologically mature organism and which he can view objectively and within the context of extensive previous experience. To the child's immature emotional and cognitive systems, the things that happen are assimilated at a much more fundamental level, and help define, for better or worse, the very meaning of being alive. A child brought up by a rejecting mother will see the world as a much more hostile place than will the child raised in happier circumstances. The child who always has to yell his head off to get attention will have a different idea of human relationships from the child whose wants are respected and satisfied. The child who is brought up in the shadow of his parents' unhappy marriage, or who constantly has demands made upon him that he is temperamentally unable to meet, will see the world as a more threatening place than will the child who enjoys more social harmony.

Though we need not dwell upon it, since there is no proof that it applies equally to humans, there is evidence that animals brought up in environmental impoverishment may even suffer physiological impairment. For example, Teyler (1975) reports evidence that rats raised in social isolation have a thinner cerebral cortex, less developed neural connections, and secrete less brain chemicals than do rats raised in a stimulating and enriched environment. Not surprisingly, the unfortunate creatures also perform less well on the kinds of discrimination problems that in humans are normally regarded as signs of intelligence. Such physiological impairment seems to be permanent. Because of their social isolation, the rats have been deprived of the possibility for physiological growth open to them during the critical period concerned.

Erikson's developmental stages

One approach to the subject of personality development is to see it as composed of a number of stages, each of them dominated by certain learning-tasks which must be completed properly if the individual is to move satisfactorily on to the next stage. One of the main proponents of this theory in the field of personality is Erik Erikson (e.g. 1971). Erikson holds that in personality there are eight critical periods, or stages, spread out over the whole of the individual's lifespan, and he defines them in terms of the positive learning that takes place if they are successfully negotiated, and the negative learning that takes place if they are not (e.g. 1959). The eight stages are given in table 1. It would be a mistake to see these stages as concrete and invariable, but they are useful to us in that they help us understand something not only of the influence of environment on personality development, but also of the way in which this influence changes as the child grows older. In the following sections, we shall therefore

Table 1   Erikson's Developmental Stages

		Positive *Negative*
1	Early infancy	trust *versus* mistrust
2	Late infancy	autonomy *versus* shame and doubt
3	Early childhood	initiative *versus* guilt
4	Middle childhood	competence *versus* inferiority
5	Adolescence	identity *versus* role confusion
6	Early adulthood	intimacy *versus* isolation
7	Middle adulthood	generativity *versus* stagnation
8	Late adulthood	self-acceptance *versus* despair

use Erikson's stages as a convenient framework for discussing the factors in personality development relevant to the teacher, though this discussion will draw upon a much wider context than simply Erikson's own work. Erikson isolated these stages as a result of his experiences in clinical psychology both in Europe and in America. However, he does not propose that these stages represent all the major learning-tasks that the individual has to face if his personality is to develop successfully. What he suggests is that they are a useful way of looking at childhood and adulthood, and of isolating the point at which the child or the adult may go astray in his development. The eight stages are by no means hard and fast ones, and, even though the individual may apparently come through each one satisfactorily, some negative learning will almost certainly take place, and may remain within the personality as a potential source of insecurity.

Erikson's ideas have proved influential in the field of education, and his eight stages provide a convenient way for us to examine personality development. Concentrating on the first six, let us take each one in turn, and discuss it within the context of the work of the teacher.

1 *Trust* versus *mistrust*   Erikson accepts the great importance of the child–mother (or mother-substitute) relationship in the first three years of life. He divides these years into his first two developmental stages, *stage one* covering the first year, and *stage two* years two and three. In year one, Erikson sees all the various aspects of good mothering as combining to produce in the child a sense of trust. From his mother's love and care and from her consistent presence as the satisfier of all his various needs, the child learns that the world around him is a place he can trust, a secure place in which he can safely consign his physical and emotional well-being to the good offices of others, in consequence becoming free to turn his attention to all the other interesting things that surround him.

Denied this sense of trust, the child may become fearful and anxious, and, dependent upon temperament, either have little energy or confidence for relating to the outside world, or feel that he must take what he wants from it by aggression and hostility.

2 *Autonomy* versus *shame and doubt* If he comes through this first stage successfully, the child's urge to reach out and explore the world is aided from the second year of life onwards by his growing physical competence. From the secure base of his trust in those around him, he sets out on a voyage of discovery. Inevitably, this voyage involves experimenting to find out the extent of his powers over the people and objects in his world, and, just as inevitably, this involves him in the increasing exercise of his own will. Many psychologists (e.g. Church 1976) testify to the child's going through a particularly negative phase during the third year of his life, in which he appears deliberately to defy those around him. If thwarted, he may show temper tantrums and be aggressive and destructive. This seems to be a necessary part of his experimentation, and a necessary sign that he is beginning to see himself as a distinct, autonomous person, differentiated from those around him. The long-term consequences of adult reaction to the child during this phase may well be considerable. If the adult meets him head on in a conflict of wills, then, dependent upon temperament, the child may become increasingly difficult, determined to make his own will prevail even at the cost of the feelings of conflict that this arouses in him, or he may abandon his attempt at asserting his autonomy, and become inhibited and full of doubts about himself.

Often it is difficult for adults to avoid this conflict of wills. The child seems to be threatening adult authority, and that's not an easy thing to take from a two-year-old; but the role of the adult should be one of patience and understanding, a role in which the child's autonomy is respected and encouraged where practicable, and limited consistently and with gentle firmness where it is not. Thus the child will learn that the world is a place in which certain laws and standards obtain, within the limits of which he can do things for himself and take decisions for himself. By learning that control is not something that is always exerted upon him from outside, he will also begin to learn that he has responsibilities for self-control. Just as he can influence the behaviour of people and things in the world around him, so he can influence his own behaviour, and gain in consequence the rewards of adult approval which such self-control brings.

Erikson sums up the stage of autonomy *versus* shame and doubt by saying that it is decisive for the ratio within the child's future behaviour of 'co-operation and wilfulness, self-expression and its suppression. From a sense of self-control comes a lasting sense of good will and pride; from a sense of loss of self-control and of foreign overcontrol comes a lasting propensity for doubt and shame.'

3 *Initiative* versus *guilt* This stage, which begins at the age of about three or four, is the first one in which the teacher is directly concerned. If the child has successfully consolidated his autonomy, he is now free to find out the extent to which he is allowed to put this autonomy to good effect. Increasing physical agility on the one hand, and increasing linguistic skills on the other, allow him to communicate more fully with the people and things around him, and to give more scope to his powers of initiative. In his expanding world, which now embraces the nursery school or the play-group as well as the home, he discovers the extent to which he can exercise this initiative, and the extent to which it is to be restricted by others.

Since this period of development also marks the growth of moral behaviour and of the conscience, such restrictions, dependent upon the language in which adults express them, may lead to the child's feeling worthless and guilty for being as he is, and for wanting to do the things that he wants to do. He is also likely to be increasingly influenced by the behaviour of those around him, in particular of those older than him. His most important models of behaviour (*role models*) are usually his parents. From both parents, but particularly from the parent of the same sex, the child also begins at this time to learn his definitive sex role. Some part of this sex role is, of course, biologically determined. Smith (1974) reviews evidence to show that in other primates besides man the male is more prone to engage in aggressive and in boisterous physical activity from infancy onwards than is the female, and that this difference disappears if the female's mother has been injected with male hormones during the pregnancy. But, whether we like it or not, a significant part of the sex role is learnt from parents, teachers and the adult world in general. For example, in our society violent activity is more readily countenanced in boys than it is in girls. Certain pastimes are regarded as boyish, certain others as girlish. Books, toys, games, even colours, are usually chosen for a child with his or her sex in mind.

What this means is that boys and girls have different kinds of limits placed upon their initiative. A boy who engages in girlish pursuits is made to feel uncomfortable and guilty about it, as is the girl who engages in boyish ones. Perhaps because of their traditional role in the home, girls have their initiative further curbed in that they are encouraged to be more dependent than boys. Lewis (1972) shows that this dependency training in girls is often evident from the second year of life onwards, and appears to continue right through into adolescence, and Davie and his colleagues (1972) show that girls are more anxious for parental approval than boys, while boys are more concerned with the approval of other children. Older siblings also help the child to learn his sex role. Koch (1956) has shown that boys with older sisters take more interest in girlish activities than do boys with only older brothers, while girls with older brothers show a corresponding interest in boyish things.

The growth of initiative has obvious implications for the kind of education that we ought to be offering to children at this stage in their lives. Assuming that we want to encourage this initiative, assuming that we want children to develop their sense of independence, assuming that we want them to grow in responsibility, and to be capable of taking decisions and of using their imagination, then the school or play-group must give children the appropriate opportunities. This means, of course, having the right kinds of equipment, the water and sand, the crayons, paints and clay, the building-blocks and the constructional toys, the climbing frame, the home corner, the cooker, the dressing-up clothes, the books, the musical instruments and the animals. But, more than any of these, it means having the right kind of relationship with children. Teachers of the very young are dedicated people, and it would be quite wrong to talk of such a thing as 'teacher neglect' analogous to parental neglect, but there is a danger that in their relationship with children teachers may unwittingly be inclined to exercise the wrong sort of control over them.

We need to enlarge on this. I wrote earlier that, dependent upon the language which adults use to enforce them, the restrictions that are laid upon a child may make him feel worthless and guilty for being as he is. Obviously, there are many things that children must be prevented from doing. What is important, though, is that the child should not be made to feel at odds with himself for wanting to do them. We shall be returning to this point of guilt and self-rejection in children when we come to discuss personality theories, particularly those of Carl Rogers, in chapter 4. But it cannot be stressed too strongly that it is very damaging for a child to be made to feel that he is wicked or bad for wanting to behave as he does. These wants may stem from deep biological drives over which the child has no control. Labels such as 'good' or 'bad' are quite inappropriate for these drives, and belong only to the way in which the child learns to control them and to channel them into socially acceptable forms.

This means that the teacher should always focus attention upon a child's action, rather than pass moral judgement upon the child himself. It is the action that is unacceptable, not the child. 'That wasn't a very kind thing to do', rather than 'You are an unkind boy.' 'That was a thoughtless thing to say', rather than 'You are a silly girl.' The child's self-concepts, as we shall see later, are immature, fragile things. He gains his idea of the kind of person he is from listening to what the adults in his life tell him about himself. If they are constantly censuring him, and thus assuring him of his lack of worth, he may incorporate this negative picture into his own self-image, and not only feel guilt in consequence, but often come to produce the very sort of anti-social behaviour that he feels adults expect of him.

The teacher, like the parents, also acts as a role model for the child. The warmer the relationship between teacher and child, the more effective a model will she be. Any discipline which relies upon harshness, or upon the constant deprival of privileges, is likely to alienate the child, and, dependent upon his temperament and home background, to frighten him, to antagonise him, or simply to make him withdraw his attention elsewhere. In all these cases, the teacher's function as an agent in the child's socialisation will be greatly diminished. The most satisfactory deterrent that the teacher has for unwanted behaviour is to withdraw her approval of it in the manner mentioned above, preferably at the same time suggesting an alternative, more acceptable activity.

As far as the child's developing sex role is concerned, it is important that all school activities should be open to both sexes, and that different standards of behaviour should not be demanded of them. However, the teacher's influence in this sphere is not all-embracing. The child will quickly learn his sex role outside school, and it would be wrong for the teacher to impose a form of unisexualism upon children that will expose them to ridicule in the home! The best that the teacher can hope for is that the child will grow up respecting the opposite sex.

4 *Competence* versus *inferiority*   Having learnt initiative, which frees the child to *do* things, he now faces the task of learning competence, which frees him to do them *well*. This stage, which lasts approximately throughout the primary-school years, is marked by the child's growing physical and linguistic skills. In a few short years he moves from the world of infancy to something approaching an adult's physical co-ordination and verbal fluency. As he does so, he vastly increases his capacity for experience. As developmental psychologists have shown us, he also builds up his cognitive skills and uses them to comprehend and manipulate this experience.

These maturing skills profoundly influence the picture he builds of his environment. He asks questions, he interprets the answers, he watches how things behave, he tackles problems, doing all these things in his own unique way. Further, not only is there a wide variation between different children, the same child has a pretty broad repertoire of responses himself. However well the teacher may know the class, she will be hard put to it to predict how individual children will react to many of the stimuli of everyday classroom life. At times, it seems as if the child is trying out different kinds of responses to the same stimulus simply to see which one works best, experimenting to see how the world behaves and to determine the extent to which his own skills allow him to influence this behaviour.

Sadly, many children by this time are already showing signs of slipping inexorably behind the others in this business of acquiring skills. Sometimes they seem innately less able to ask the right kind of questions, and to comprehend the answers when they come. Sometimes they seem to have missed the kinds of stimulation that we have been talking about in the last chapter and in this. Failing to gain trust, autonomy or initiative – or sometimes all three – the child is handicapped in his attempts to make use of his innate potential. The older he becomes, the worse things often get. His failure to master early skills renders him less able to master later ones. Failure, like success, breeds upon itself. With each experience of failure, he becomes less and less sure of himself, less and less ready to tackle new things, less and less confident of his own abilities. Conversely, the child who is developing competence has the constant reassurance that his skills are an effective way of dealing with the world, and of keeping a balance between its demands and his own needs. With this competence comes an increasing conviction of the world's consistency and predictability, and of his own status and prestige within it. He develops a defined personality, within an environment which he comprehends. And, as he watches and identifies with his teachers and his parents, so he can see that his own skills are a successful version of the way in which they themselves go about the business of living.

During the primary-school years, the child discovers other role models besides his parents and teachers, of course. And this discovery highlights more sharply than ever his developing competence, or the lack of it. From now on he begins increasingly to discover these models amongst other children, and becomes aware of their levels of competence in relation to his own. Other children do things better or worse than he does, other children get better or worse marks, get more or less praise from the teacher, are more or less popular with the rest of the class, get into trouble more or less often. And whether we like it or not, as teachers we help this process of comparison. We draw attention to good work, we withhold approval from bad, we assign classroom jobs, we give extra help. The very uniqueness of children makes it impossible to treat them all alike.

In the last section I described the effect that the teacher can have upon the child's feelings of guilt and self-rejection. Unfortunately, little research has been carried out on the influence that teachers have on the child's concepts of competence and mastery. But significant evidence of the role which parents play in this area comes from the work of Stanley Coopersmith in the USA. Coopersmith (e.g. 1968) followed a group of boys through from age ten to early adult life, and found that, on the basis of psychological tests and of self and teacher ratings, they divided consistently throughout into three groups which he labelled high, medium and low self-esteem. High self-esteem boys were from the beginning active and expressive; they enjoyed joining in, and were generally successful academically and socially. They were confident, not unduly worried by criticism, and had an accurate picture of their own abilities. Medium self-esteem boys shared many of these qualities, but were more conformist, more anxious for social acceptance, and less sure of their own worth. The low self-esteem boys were, by contrast, what Coopersmith calls a sad little group, isolated, fearful, self-conscious, reluctant to participate, and very sensitive to criticism. They were prone to underrate themselves, and were preoccupied with their own problems.

What was of particular interest was that membership of these three groups did not appear to be particularly correlated with physical attractiveness, intelligence or affluence (all came from middle-class homes). But in examining their backgrounds Coopersmith found that the high self-esteem boys came from homes in which they were regarded as significant and interesting people, and in which their views on family decisions were invited and listened to. Parental expectations were more consistent and were higher than in the other two groups, and discipline was less permissive, though it depended more upon rewards than withdrawal of love or upon corporal punishment. The boys praised their parents' fairness. The low self-esteem boys, on the other hand, often rated their parents as unfair. There was little sign that their parents were interested in them or gave them clear guidance, and standards of discipline were inconsistent, veering unpredictably from extreme permissiveness to extreme strictness.

These findings are of interest to teachers not only for the light which they throw on children's backgrounds, but also because they can be applied equally well to the classroom. The high self-esteem boys were generally successful in what they did, set themselves high goals, and worked more nearly to their potential, because they were not inhibited by the fear of failure, or by uncertainties as to their worth. If one has a realistic knowledge of, and confidence in, one's own skills, one is less wounded by the occasional failure, less deflated by the odd criticism, less anxious for the unqualified approval of all and sundry. One is readier to participate, less overawed by things, less daunted by possible pressures. The high self-esteem boys knew they counted as people because their parents, directly and indirectly, told them so. By the same token, the teacher can show her children that they count. She can encourage them to use their abilities, urge them on when they fail instead of punishing this failure by word or deed, take a close interest in their day-to-day progress, share their pleasure in success. It is one of the golden rules of the remedial teacher that the classroom must be so structured that each child can experience this success, no matter how low his personal level of ability happens to be, and the same rule should apply with equal strength in the normal classroom.

Interestingly, the high self-esteem boys had parents who set standards, and applied them consistently, and who were not unduly permissive. I have already mentioned the importance of consistency when dealing with children, and this is perhaps the point at which I should give it particular stress. It is through his experience of consistency in others that the child gradually learns that the world is a predictable place, and that the skills acquired today will be of some value tomorrow as well. The infant's sense of trust, the older child's sense of self-esteem, are both based upon the security of knowing that the things in the world around us have patterns and laws. Water isn't dry today and wet tomorrow. People aren't kind to you one minute and cruel the next. The presence of standards in the classroom, standards that are related to the individual child's potential, gives the child a pattern against which to measure his own progress, something to aim for, proof of his own growing competence.

By setting standards, the teacher emphasises even further to children her interest in them. In all walks of life, if we are interested in anything, whether it be gardening or the local football team, we usually show this interest by a concern for standards of performance. Our garden, or mine at least, will never be like Kew, and our football team may never win the European Cup, but nevertheless, within the limits of what are possible, we have standards for them. An absence of any standards is often an indication that the thing, or the person, concerned is really not worth bothering about. In the classroom, the presence of standards shows the child that we believe in him and want to see him make progress, and shows him also that the thing we are asking him to do, the skill we are asking him to master, the knowledge we are asking him to acquire, is worth something as well.

None of this implies an absence of classroom democracy. It is significant that the high self-esteem boys came from homes in which they were encouraged to express their views, were consulted over family decisions, and were generally made to feel that they were important people. The boys praised, remember, their parents' fairness. Nor does it imply a harsh discipline. Parents relied upon encouragement rather than upon corporal punishment or the withdrawal of love. The withdrawal of love, or in the teacher's case the withdrawal of concern and of interest, are never likely to produce self-esteem in a child. He needs to feel that he matters enough to be always given these things, and that they are no more subject to change or withdrawal than are the natural laws that make the world a reliable place in which to live.

At the risk of extending this section too far, there are three other factors that have bearing upon the development of competence in a child. The first is sex. We have already looked at some of the differences in personality between boys and girls, and there is ample evidence to show that these differences are reflected in academic achievement. One of the most exhaustive longitudinal studies ever carried out, that of Davie and his colleagues (1972), shows that girls tend to talk earlier than boys, and to remain more verbally fluent than boys even after starting school. Perhaps because of this fluency, they are generally more successful than boys in learning to read. Even though the gap between the sexes has narrowed by the age of nine, there are known to be more backward readers amongst boys than amongst girls at all stages of compulsory schooling. Girls are also less likely than boys to suffer speech defects, are less likely to be accident-prone (at least outside the home), and are less likely to be referred for special help to the child-guidance clinic. Boys on the other hand are generally better at number work than are girls, and they tend to take a wider interest in events outside the home, and in how things are made and in how they work.

The precise reasons for these differences between the sexes are not known. Girls may, for cultural reasons, spend more time in the home and in conversation with their mothers than do boys, and they may spend more time in reading because they have fewer outlets in organised sport. We have seen from the reference to Davie's work in the last section that they are more anxious to please their parents, and this again may mean that they spend more time with them, and more time doing the things of which parents approve, such as school learning. But there are probably genetic reasons as well. In many areas, girls seem to mature physically more rapidly than boys, and this may mean that they are able to tackle certain skills at an earlier age than are boys.

The second factor that still needs to be mentioned is social class. One gap in the work of Coopersmith is that his sample consisted only of boys from middle-class homes. It tells us nothing about self-esteem in so-called working-class children. However, evidence from elsewhere (see, for instance, Mussen, Conger and Kagan 1984) tells us that these children, especially boys, are generally lower in self-esteem than are those from the middle class. And, if we return to Davie's work again, we find that both working-class girls and boys show more of the personality characteristics normally associated with low self-esteem, such as aggression, withdrawal, depression, and hostility to adults, than do middle-class children. Davie also shows that, for all the areas of competence in school which he tested (oral skills, creativity, reading and number work), working-class children trail significantly behind their more socially favoured peers. The inescapable conclusion is that working-class children are handicapped in their search for competence, doubtless by the higher level of maternal and paternal deprivation, the poorer amenities and facilities, the less clearly defined standards and values, that go with membership of their class.

We have to be careful here of course. It would be quite wrong to suggest that *all* working-class children have poor backgrounds, or that *all* middle-class children come from stimulating and loving homes. Many working-class homes are excellent, and many middle-class homes are barren alike of material and of emotional support. Coopersmith, remember, found many low self-esteem boys in middle-class homes. It would also be wrong to suggest that middle-class values are in all cases *better* than working-class ones. All we are saying is that the incidence of deprivation is statistically higher in working-class homes than in middle-class ones, and that middle-class values are closer to most of those that lead to success in school and in society generally. It is up to the reader to decide whether this is a good or a bad thing.

The third factor to which brief reference must be made is family size. Back in the 1930s, the psychoanalyst Alfred Adler put forward the theory that family size and one's birth order within the family have a significant influence upon personality. Adler's theory was a somewhat elaborate and fanciful one, but some part of it at least seems to be supported by modern research. Several studies, most recently Davie's, show an inverse relationship between family size and both school attainment and personality adjustment. Since this relationship holds good irrespective of social class, it rather looks as if the unavoidably reduced amount of parental attention, guidance and verbal communication which the individual often receives in a large family has a deleterious effect upon a wide range of his behaviour. This effect becomes increasingly noticeable as family size increases beyond two children. Davie also noticed that in these families it seems to be the oldest child's school attainment and social adjustment that are the most heavily penalised, presumably because, being the oldest, he is left to fend for himself by the parents more than are any of the others.

Before we leave the question of competence and personality development, perhaps I could take up just one point mentioned a few paragraphs ago. I said that, amongst other things, a high level of *hostility to adults* is a characteristic of some children, particularly working-class children, who are low on self-esteem. This might seem strange, but the reason for it is not hard to seek. If a child finds that in everything he does in the school and at home he is reminded of the fact that he is just not as good as most other children of his age, he can either accept this knowledge and become one of the sad little children to whom Coopersmith refers, or he can try to protect what is left of his self-esteem by fighting back. If he is no good at the things he is asked to do at school, he can either accept that this means *he* is no good, or he can reject the things themselves, and announce to the world, with hostility or with bravado, that *they* are not worth doing. If he fails to measure up to the standards of the school, he is in effect saying it is not he who is incompetent; it is the standards that are wrong.

5 *Identity* versus *role confusion*   Erikson sees all the stages through which the personality passes in its development as really

stages in self-discovery. By finding out about his place in the world, by listening to what other people have to say about him, by identifying with adults and with other children, by comparing himself with his peers, the child gradually builds up a picture of the person he is. He forms an *identity*. This process comes to a head in adolescence, and although the personality may go on developing throughout adult life, the more successfully the individual weathers the crisis of adolescence, the more sure and realistic is he likely to be as a young adult, and the clearer and better defined his identity. Should the individual fail in the self-discovery tasks that face him in adolescence, he will suffer from what Erikson calls *role confusion*. He will have no clear idea of the person he is, and become a prey to the many diverse and conflicting pressures of adult life, clinging for security to a rigid and artificial picture of himself that leaves no room for change.

The most important biological feature of adolescence is the arrival of physical and sexual maturity. This abrupt transition from childhood to adulthood can cause all kinds of problems. It takes girls approximately four years, from the onset of the adolescent growth spurt at about age twelve and a half, to reach adult stature, with boys starting and finishing about eighteen months later. The adolescent has learned to cope with the business of being a child; now he finds himself called upon to cope with the business of being an adult, and to cope with it in a complex industrial society which, partly because of the lateness of the school-leaving age, is reluctant to accord him adult status. More primitive societies than ours, where the child is automatically granted the rights and responsibilities of adulthood at puberty, appear to experience far fewer problems with this age group than we do. Sociologists have suggested that these problems are therefore more a product of our 'artificial' culture than of the biological changes of adolescence itself.

Be that as it may, there is no denying that these problems exist. Obviously, they vary in intensity from individual to individual, but most adolescents find that many of the concepts which they have built up during childhood seem suddenly outdated. What they now have to learn is whether the naughty boy necessarily becomes the bad man, whether the good boy necessarily becomes the good one. Naughtiness, which once may have seemed a downright nuisance to one's peers, may now come to be regarded by them as an admirable rejection of authority, while goodness may come to be seen as a furtive attempt to gain adult favours. To make matters worse, partly because of changes in hormonal balance, many adolescents are prone to wildly fluctuating moods. Love and affection towards those around them may suddenly change to irritation and even active dislike. Not surprisingly, this causes the adolescent great perplexity (to say nothing of what it causes to the adults in his life!) Who, hidden within this confusion, is the real person?

To complicate things still further, the adolescent often finds himself taking on the colour of his surroundings. He behaves one way with his friends, another way with his parents, another way with his teachers. Each of these ways seems to involve a quite different set of values, and to impose quite different demands upon him. If he belongs to a minority group, such as an immigrant community or a minority social group, these conflicting demands may be even worse. And, whoever he is, he often seems to be faced with having to make important decisions without clear guidance, because there appears to be no experienced person who really understands his position.

Intellectually, the majority of adolescents manifest what Piaget calls the stage of *formal operations*, a stage in cognitive development characterised by an increased use of abstract and deductive reasoning, and it is this, together with his frustration at the adult world, that often makes the adolescent so prone to question things. Abstract concepts such as freedom, justice and equality take on a deeper meaning for him, and before the realities of adult life catch up with him he often goes through a phase of intense idealism during which he wants to set the world to rights. It is partly this that often makes him espouse political and social causes, but there is another reason too: namely, that in spite of his outward assurance, the adolescent is frequently far from certain that his opinions, particularly when they are at variance with his teachers' or parents', are really correct. The doubts that he has over his own identity stretch to these as well. He is still experimenting with himself, still trying out his adult clothes so to speak, and by supporting causes and joining things he experiences a sense of kinship that gives him confidence. If other people are rebelling against authority, and are prepared to let him become one of them, then he reasons that his personal battles against teachers and parents must be justified too.

The adolescent's partial rejection of the authority of his parents and teachers also makes him less inclined than hitherto to see them as role models. He finds alternatives, sometimes in cult heroes such as sportsmen and pop stars, sometimes in his peer group. Indeed, the peer group becomes increasingly important to him, especially in matters of dress, speech and behaviour. Acceptance by the peer group is of great moment to him. He finds himself excessively concerned to conform to its norms, excessively on show to it in all he does. He may be acutely embarrassed by anything, such as late physical development, which sets him apart from these norms. The sex drive, which in males appears to reach its peak at about sixteen to eighteen years of age, also makes the adolescent take an increasing interest in the opposite sex, and to be unsuccessful in relationships with it may be a profound blow to both boys and girls, and may lead to negative self-concepts that will crucially affect decisions later in life about such things as vocation, friends, lifestyle and marriage partner.

Adolescence is also a peak age for delinquent activity. Although delinquency, as we have already suggested, is a multi-causal phenomenon, whose origins stretch back into faulty adjustment early in childhood, the majority of delinquent acts tend to occur in children who are in or near the final year of compulsory schooling, precisely the time when they are most irked by their continuing lack of adult status. Their lower levels of aggression, their greater dependency, their more effective socialisation, and their earlier reconciliation to their role in life make girls less prone to delinquent activity than are boys, though over recent years delinquent acts in girls, particularly those involving violence, have been increasing proportionately faster than in boys (in America the ratio of one such act in girls to every five in boys is now reported to be down to one to three). This is probably a reflection of the changing status of women in our society.

Evidence from both Britain and America suggests that the personality of the delinquent adolescent is characterised by hostility, suspicion, impulsiveness and low self-control. Usually there are poor self-concepts, feelings of inadequacy and rejection, and of confusion and conflict (see, for instance, Conger and

Miller 1966). In addition to maternal deprivation, parents of delinquents usually show those characteristics noticed by Coopersmith in the family background of low self-esteem boys: that is, they are erratic, unpredictable and show little evidence of any genuine interest in children. Frequently the father is rejected as a role model by the son because of the father's weakness, drunkenness or harshness. The incidence of delinquency increases sharply as we move down the social classes, and typically the delinquent comes from a deprived urban area, where, as we saw in chapter 1, elements in the community may approve such values as toughness and a rejection of authority.

In delinquency there is probably also a temperamental factor at work. I mentioned in chapter 1 that Glueck and Glueck have found a high proportion of mesomorphs amongst delinquents, and it may be that the high leadership and aggressive qualities that mesomorphs have, when denied socially acceptable outlets, turn to the gang sub-culture which features so prominently in delinquent activity. Further evidence for a temperamental factor comes from the work of Eysenck, who finds that delinquent samples are significantly extroverted, which again suggests a high level of aggression and an innate need for external stimuli and excitement (see chapter 5).

Enough of the negative side of adolescence. It is not difficult to make adolescence seem a somewhat unattractive stage in human development. But in fact many teachers much prefer working with this age group, and welcome the adolescent's potential for idealism and involvement. They also find it exciting to watch the personality develop in such a brief span from a childish to an adult one, and find great reward from the help that they can give to the process. Part of their secret in dealing successfully with adolescents is that they seem aware of the experimental nature of much of what the adolescent does. By their tolerance, but at the same time by the clear and consistent standards which they maintain in areas where such standards are not negotiable, they help the adolescent to answer the questions which he is posing of his environment, and to understand the limits that exist in the new grown-up world that he is about to enter.

They also seem aware of the depths of feeling and the vulnerability that underlie the sometimes brash and cynical adolescent exterior. Faced with the problem of achieving an identity in which the various parts of his personality enter into a consistent relationship with each other and are not lost in role confusion, the adolescent feels profound self-doubts, and needs the security of knowing that his teacher has confidence in the kind of person that he is becoming. The brashness and the cynicism are often no more than a defensive screen, erected to hide inner sensitivities and to impress the peer group. The good teacher sees through the screen, though she is careful not to puncture it, particularly in front of the rest of the class, because this kind of humiliation can only lead to shame and loss of face for the adolescent, and often to a subsequent unforgiving hostility towards the teacher.

Teachers who understand adolescents also seem aware of the continuing need to show an interest – though never an intrusive one – in the adolescent's activities. This means his activities outside school as well as inside, and in his future prospects and ambitions as well as in his present performance. Such teachers also show an interest in his likes and dislikes. They listen to and respect his opinions, they tolerate his desire to be different from his elders, and they don't make glib judgements about his personality from such externals as fashions in appearance, speech or dress. They encourage him to bring into the classroom as a fit subject for discussion his problems over personal and sexual relationships, and they are prepared to give clear answers to his questions, and to indicate the difference in the field of values between fact and belief, both of which have their place but which involve different kinds of issues.

They also understand the conflict, now often brought into sharper focus than ever in some children's lives, between the standards of school and those of the home. Any direct conflict between home and school can greatly increase the pressures towards role confusion in the child. Often the school can best reconcile these pressures by avoiding the unnecessary rules and restrictions which give the child the impression that school is out of touch with the real world. In any community, rules are necessary if people are to live together in harmony, but these rules should exist clearly and obviously for that end, and not to serve outmoded customs, or the prejudices of one small group. The more democratic the process that can be used to arrive at rules, the more point everyone sees in them, and the more likely they are to be obeyed. Bad rules, which are inevitably ignored as soon as those responsible for them have their backs turned, lead only to a loss of respect for authority, and a consequent flouting of many other rules that are there for a much better purpose (see, for instance, Fontana 1985a).

There is some evidence that by a policy of rejecting the least able children in its own midst, a school can also cause its own kinds of conflicts and sub-cultures. Rigid setting and streaming by ability, for example, can lead to what have been called 'A' and 'C' stream mentalities, the former characterised by acceptance of the school, of its staff, and of its values, and the latter by their rejection. This is not the place to enter the debate about streaming, which has implications beyond those associated with personality, but the point is that, where schools feel the need to separate children by ability, this should be done in a way which protects the self-esteem of the less able as well as of the more able.

Finally, teachers who work well with adolescents seem to understand that it is no good looking for the obedience and dependency in them which they had when younger. It is a failure to show this understanding that leads to many of the conflicts which parents have with adolescent sons and daughters. Refusal to accept that the adolescent is growing up only makes him assert his right to independence all the more strongly. Teachers who recognise this right take care to give him every reasonable opportunity to demonstrate his growing ability to take adult responsibility. Such opportunities are of far more value than any number of homilies directed at him by the adults in his life on the *need* for him to develop this responsibility. Too often when we lecture adolescents, and indeed younger children, on the desirability of their acquiring a maturer approach to life, we mean that they should acquire it only when it suits us, and at other times revert to the subordination of an earlier stage in their development. This is a misguided practice, and perhaps if we all realised it we should have less reason in education to bemoan the 'irresponsibility' of the young.

6 *Intimacy* versus *isolation*   This stage, which occurs in early adulthood, is more the direct concern of teachers involved in higher and further education, but it is of relevance to all teachers

in that it is the culmination of the years of childhood and adolescence. Intimacy is the ability to have full and satisfying personal relationships with other people of both sexes, relationships which culminate in marriage, in lifelong friendships, and in close and sustaining contacts with the people with whom one works, and with the people in one's community.

Perhaps the best way of discussing this stage is to merge it with the wider discussion of the mature personality: that is, with a discussion of those personal qualities that mark people out as having attained a balance and a richness in their development that allows them to live full and satisfying lives. Erikson has himself written widely on the mature personality, but the psychologist who has centred most attention on it is probably Gordon Allport (1897–1967). Allport (1961) sees the acquisition of a real sense of personal identity in adolescence as meaning that the individual has developed from being essentially a number of different people to being a single, or whole, person. In the early stages of our personality development, Allport sees us as possessing a wide range of 'traits' such as friendliness, honesty, bookishness, which we use somewhat inconsistently and arbitrarily in our dealings with other people (e.g. we are honest with our friends but not with our teachers, bookish at school but not at home). As we grow older, many of these coalesce into a smaller number of better integrated units which Allport calls *selves* (e.g. we have one recognisable self for school, another for home), and, with the discovery of identity, these come together in turn to form the single unit of the mature personality.

To Allport, the mature personality is, therefore, characterised by co-ordination and consistency. If a person is mature, we know that whatever the situation in which we meet him he remains identifiably the same person (within reasonable limits at least; every personality may break down under extreme stress). He is not honest at home and dishonest at work (or honest and dishonest at both home and work in different circumstances), or pious at church and amoral at the local club, or humorous with his friends and a wet blanket with his family, or confident with men but a pitiful stammerer with women. He does not, in fact, still have several different selves, each one of them capable of its own separate codes of behaviour and of values. An extreme example of people who had failed to achieve this mature integration were those Nazi concentration-camp officers who were reputedly good husbands and fathers in the evenings, but spent their days sending innocent people to a hideous death.

Of course, this is not all there is to maturity. Usually when we talk of the mature personality we imply a value judgement in that we expect his integrated personality to have qualities that make him desirable to the community as a whole. It is possible, in theory at least, for a person to be entirely integrated in doing evil, which might mean that he meets Allport's criterion, but is hardly the sort of person we should want to have as a neighbour or as a teacher of children. We also usually think of the mature person as being an effective person, as being good at getting things done within his chosen field. This is supported by such studies as those of Barron (1954), who found that graduate students rated most highly on maturity of personality by their teachers seemed to be particularly good at organising their work, at judging themselves and others, and at resisting stress. They also seemed to be high on integrity, and to be energetic, adaptable, resourceful and well adjusted (see also Barron 1979).

Allport recognizes the need for a definition of maturity which takes into account these questions of value and, in summarising the views of a number of psychologists on the subject, he suggests that the mature personality manifests the following qualities:

1 An extended sense of self, allowing him to transcend the self-centredness of childhood, and to identify with the concerns and problems of others.

2 A warm relationship with others, allowing him to love them for their own sakes as well as for his own.

3 Emotional security, allowing him to withstand the problems and fears of daily life.

4 Self-insight, allowing him to laugh at himself without loss of self-esteem. (There is *some* correlation between self-insight and intelligence, though the one by no means necessarily implies the other.)

5 A realistic orientation towards the world, allowing him to exercise sound judgement of people and things, and to take necessary decisions.

6 A unifying philosophy of life, either religious or humanistic, allowing him to interpret life's purpose and to decide on long-term goals and on standards of behaviour.

This makes the mature person sound like a paragon of perfection, but this is misleading. A respect for others, for example, does not stop him from sometimes feeling angry or impatient with them. Sound judgement does not mean that he never makes a mistake. Emotional security does not mean he never feels depressed or inadequate. Self-insight does not mean he never feels surprised at himself, or never feels disappointment at failing to achieve a cherished ambition. The basic point about maturity is that the mature person is not constantly at the mercy of his own weaknesses, or constantly vulnerable to people and events in the world outside. He has a degree of self-knowledge and self-control that allow him to make the most of himself, a respect for those close to him that allows him to love them without smothering them, a tolerance for the world in general that allows him to respect the rights of others, and a sense of purpose and of aspiration that give substance and direction to his life.

Many of these qualities may not develop, of course, until the individual is well past early adulthood. The personality still has to face major problems of learning and of adaptation in middle and later life. Erikson describes these as *generativity*, which is the ability to innovate, to bring in new ideas, and, in particular, to influence the next generation through parenthood and teaching, and as *self-acceptance* – that is, the ability to review one's life in old age with a sense of fulfilment, with a knowledge that one has done what one could to enhance the lives of others and to use productively whatever abilities one was fortunate enough to possess.

It is a pity that we can't take up these points, particularly those that relate to later life, and develop them more fully. The majority of the years in a man's life lie outside the formal educational process, and from the point of view of personality growth and adjustment this is unfortunate. People often face major problems of adaptation in middle and later life which education is allowed to do little about. The middle-aged mother who finds her children have grown up and left her, the man in his fifties who finds himself locked in a profoundly unsatisfying job and way of life, the retired couple who have more leisure than they know how to use – for all of these, formal education should be a lifelong process. If it were, it would make this book a very much longer one, but it would shorten the list of those needing medical help for problems that owe more to depression and to a sense of personal inadequacy and futility than to organic illness.

3

Psychodynamic Approaches to Personality

We have looked at the determinants and the development of personality, and it is now time that we turned our attention to the nature of personality itself. That is, to the processes within the individual that go to make up what we call personality, and to the way in which these processes interact with each other and with the environment. Psychologists have put forward various descriptions and explanations of these processes, often in sharp conflict with each other, but in the following chapters I shall attempt to show how many of these descriptions and explanations carry, in their different ways, considerable practical implications for the teacher.

We can start by looking at what is called the *idiographic* approach, which holds that, since each person is unique, personality can best be studied by in-depth investigations of individuals or of small groups. Idiographic theories originate mainly in clinical psychology, where the psychologist (or psychiatrist, if he happens to be a medically qualified psychologist) works with people suffering from personality problems, such as excessive anxiety, which make it hard for them to cope with even the ordinary stresses of everyday life. From the educational point of view their interest lies in the fact they provide us with models that may help us understand something of the motivating forces that underlie human behaviour, particularly where these processes are linked to so-called unconscious factors. The best-known idiographic theories are those which are given the general title of *psychodynamic theories*.

Many writers (e.g. Hall and Lindzey 1970) see modern psychology as dominated by three schools of thought: *psychodynamics*, *behaviourism*, and, more recently, *humanistic psychology*, the last two of which we look at in subsequent chapters. The logical point at which to start a discussion of psychodynamics is with Sigmund Freud.

Sigmund Freud

If one had to make a list of those people whose thinking has most radically altered the way in which Western man views himself, Freud's name would occupy a prominent place. The founding father of psychoanalysis, the most influential of the various psychodynamic schools, Freud (1856–1939) was born of Jewish stock in Moravia in Czechoslovakia, but lived most of his life in Vienna until forced to flee to London in 1938 to escape Nazi persecution. During his fertile career he published so many books and papers (his collected works run to twenty-four volumes in the standard edition), introduced so many theories and ideas, and fought so many battles with his fellow psychologists, that it is never easy to know where to begin an account of his work. Further, since Freud was constantly refining and developing his theories, it is sometimes hard to sort one's way through the apparent contradictions in his writings.

Nowadays many of Freud's theories are accepted in their literal form only by the most devoted of his disciples, but his influence has been such that many of his concepts are in everyday use not only by psychologists but by laymen as well, and the same holds for much of his language. Indeed, perhaps no other psychologist's work has sunk more deeply into the texture of our national culture. For the teacher, Freud's main contribution is that he gave us a new way of looking at childhood in stark contrast to the belief that misbehaviour and other personality problems in children are the invariable result of wilfulness to be corrected by stern and rigid discipline. To Freud, the child is very much more sinned against by the adult world than sinning, very much more a victim of the mistakes of his parents than of mistakes of his own making. But Freud did more than simply focus attention upon childhood experiences. He suggested that the way in which these experiences influence later personality development can only be understood if we explore the unconscious as well as the conscious mind. Belief in the power of the unconscious mind to determine human behaviour is now so widespread that it can come as a surprise to know how different things were before Freud. Freud did not originate the idea of the unconscious, which has been with us since antiquity; but to most psychologists before Freud the unconscious was simply a 'waste paper basket of ideas and memories which had fallen below the threshold of awareness because they were relatively unimportant and lacked the mental energy to force their way into consciousness' (Brown 1964).

Freud took precisely the opposite view. After qualifying as a medical doctor at the University of Vienna in 1881, Freud's interest in nervous disorders took him to work first with the hypnotist Charcot in France, and later with Joseph Breuer back in Vienna. It was during this time that he became convinced that human behaviour has a source much deeper than the conscious mind. Breuer had devised what he called a 'talking out' technique, in which the patient's nervous disorders – such as fears, phobias, irrational anxieties – were much improved simply by talking about them to the physician, and adding any additional memories and thoughts which happened to come into his or her head at the same time. Freud was very impressed with the effectiveness of this technique, and, as he had become increasingly dissatisfied with hypnosis, he experimented with it himself extensively. Eventually he developed from it what is now called the technique of *free association*. In free association the patient is invited to report, without reservation, the thoughts which come to mind in response to stimulus words or ideas presented to him or her by the psychologist (or *psychoanalyst* as the Freudian psychologist is more correctly called). The theory is that gradually, through one thought leading to another, the patient will involuntarily recall memories of the events which led to the development of present nervous disorders.

It was the astonishingly complex network of thoughts and recollections which his patients revealed during free association, many of them stretching back into early childhood and apparently long since forgotten, that convinced Freud that the conscious mind is only the tip of the iceberg of mental life, with the more important part lying beneath the waters of unconsciousness. Far from it being simply a 'waste paper basket of ideas and memories', the unconscious is, he felt, the main impulse behind human behaviour, energised by profound instinctual drives. And, far from lacking the mental energy to force themselves into consciousness, Freud saw the contents of the unconscious as kept out of awareness precisely because their significance and power form too great a threat to man's precarious socialised self.

To understand this part of Freud's theory, we must remember that he was writing at a time when deterministic ideas were gaining strength in the scientific world. Everything had to have a cause, a source of energy, which produced its visible effects. In the case of human psychology, it seemed to Freud that the unconscious was this cause. The powerful instinctive drives that his patients revealed in their unconscious during free association convinced him that this was the dynamo (hence the term *psychodynamic psychology*) that provided the motivational energy for all mental activity. True, in the course of man's evolution the unconscious has become overlaid with the thin veneer of civilised thinking that we call the conscious mind, but the conscious mind has no mental energy of its own. Within the dynamic system of human psychology, energy has to be transferred continually from the unconscious to the conscious if the latter is to function. As we shall see shortly, it is when there is breakdown in the orderly way in which this energy transfer takes place that personality problems arise.

Although Freud remained satisfied for most of his career with this division of the mind into the unconscious and the conscious, in 1922, at the age of twenty-six, he published 'The Ego and the Id', which proposed a new division of the mind, into three systems, with the terms 'unconscious' and 'conscious' now used only to describe the kinds of mental phenomena which each of these systems contains. We need to discuss these three systems, the *id*, the *ego* and the *super-ego*, separately.

The id   At birth, Freud claimed that the mind consists only of the id. The id contains everything psychological that we inherit, a fixed amount of mental or 'psychic' energy. This energy is in the form of *instincts*, i.e. of irrational drives whose only aim is to seek gratification for the individual's basic, animalistic needs.

Since the newborn baby is therefore psychologically on the level of an animal, the baby is literally an 'it' (Latin *id*) rather than a person.

As the id remains the only source of psychic energy throughout life, man can never free himself entirely from its power. The id is the primitive side of man, the 'dark force' that novelists such as D. H. Lawrence wrote about. The id links him, through the long chain of evolutionary history, with the basic forms of life from which he has arisen. Since the id is entirely unconscious, we are never directly aware of it, but it is always there, seeking the satisfaction of its powerful needs. Beneath the reach of consciousness, and of ethical and rational thought, the id can never be other than a blind, unsocialised, amoral force. Left unbridled, its drive towards selfish satisfaction would reduce human behaviour to that of the beasts.

Freud considered that the instincts within the id fall into two groups, *eros* instincts and *thanatos* instincts. The eros instincts are the life wish, and consist both of those drives directed towards self-preservation (flight, hunger, thirst, etc.) and towards preservation of the species (the sex drive, or *libido*). The thanatos instincts are the death wish, and take the form both of aggression directed outwards towards others, and of aggression directed inwards towards the self.

Freud referred to the instinctive drives of the id as *primary processes*, while the selfish objectives of these drives he termed the *pleasure principle*. During the first year or so of his life, the child is entirely dominated by the primary processes and by the pleasure principle. He lives only for the satisfaction of his primitive needs, and is unconcerned for the convenience or the wishes of other people, as many a parent dragged from the depths of slumber in the small hours of the morning by a baby's crying knows only too well. Presumably, if the small baby went on having all needs instantly gratified, he would go on being dominated by the id throughout life, but, thankfully for the rest of us, he gradually comes to realise that not all these needs are exactly in tune with reality. People don't come running every time you cry, a bottle of milk isn't always enough to satisfy you, and the discomfort of colic won't disappear just because you want it to.

In consequence, in a process which Freud never fully succeeded in explaining, part of the id begins to learn a more rational way of looking at things, and gradually separates itself off from the rest of the id to form what Freud called the ego. The socialisation of the baby has begun.

The ego   From the second year of life onwards the ego becomes an increasingly important part of the child's mental functioning. It serves as the mediator between the needs of the id and the restrictions which reality places upon the gratification of these needs. Unlike the id, which obeys the pleasure principle, the ego therefore obeys the *reality principle*. It contains all the child's rational thinking, sense of self, and all conscious thoughts. By means of the ego, the child becomes more of a person and less of an animal (*ego* = 'I'). Freud called ego processes *secondary processes* to distinguish them from the primary processes of the id. Because these secondary processes prove successful in mediating with the outside world, and in seeing to it that the id's needs are satisfied wherever possible, the id allows the ego to siphon off more and more of its psychological energy, until soon the ego has a surplus which it can turn to more creative pursuits such as the development of general interests and skills. However, the id always remains ready to cut off the flow of energy to the ego and to reassert itself should the latter fail in its primary task of satisfying the id's needs. To put it somewhat melodramatically, the animal in us always lurks just under the surface ready to take over if more civilised means fail to gratify its drives (a point which has been exploited to good effect by many a science-fiction writer, to say nothing of such novelists of childhood as William Golding in *the Lord of the Flies*).

To Freud, the diversion of energy from the id to the ego is the major dynamic event of personality development. However, it is not the final event. From the age of about six onwards, part of the child's ego separates itself off in turn and becomes the third system of the mind, the super-ego.

The super-ego   One of the ways in which the ego learns about reality is by identifying itself with other people, particularly with parents (we have already had something to say about this in the previous chapters). In the process of this identification, the child takes over many of the moral precepts of the adults in his life. But these moral precepts often owe far more to the beliefs and prejudices of these adults than they do to reality, and therefore they cannot be accommodated within the ego itself, which obeys only the reality principle. A section of the ego therefore has to break away to deal with them, and this becomes what Freud called the super-ego.

The super-ego is a very important concept in Freudian theory. It will be remembered that in chapter 2 it was said that the child gets his idea of his own moral worth largely from what people tell him about himself. Freud would claim that the super-ego provides us with a model of the mechanics of all this. Since the super-ego is created in response to the code of restrictions, admonishments and moral precepts that the parents impose upon the child, it also acquires parental powers of reward and punishment. It rewards by the feelings of pride that he gets when he obeys its promptings and strives towards the *ideal self* that it holds up as a model in front of him, and it punishes by the pangs of *conscience* that he feels when he disobeys them.

The contents of the super-ego are part conscious, but mainly unconscious. Thus most of it, like the id, lies beyond the range of rational thought. The child is saddled with many of his parents' beliefs, and finds it difficult, even as he grows older, to isolate them and submit them to rational scrutiny and debate. Thus often he behaves in certain ways because he considers them to be 'right', but is unable to give a reasoned, objective argument as to why they are right. As we shall see shortly, if the super-ego contains too many of these irrational beliefs, and becomes, as Freud put it, 'overdeveloped', it can cause almost as many personality problems to the individual as can an unchecked id. However, a normal, well-balanced super-ego is an essential part of the socialisation of the child, and the essential repository of a moral sense in us all.

By the time a child reaches the middle year in the infant school, the three personality systems of id, ego and super-ego are therefore in existence. For the personality to remain healthy, Freud considered it vital that these three systems remain in balance, with a smooth transfer of energy from id to ego to super-ego. Where the balance is disturbed, and where one of the systems dominates the others and uses up more than its fair share of this energy, the result is that the personality breaks down into excessive anxiety. Since any one of the three systems can dominate, this means that we can have three distinct forms of anxiety, *neurotic*, *realistic* or *moral*.

Neurotic anxiety   In neurotic anxiety, it is the id that dominates, and the ego, the conscious mind, goes in fear of being overwhelmed by its dark, instinctive forces. Since these forces, as we have seen, are below the level of consciousness, the person who is in the grip of neurotic anxiety is not aware of the fundamental cause of his problems. He feels his anxiety as a vague, nameless dread, a 'free-floating' anxiety that persists even when his outer life is devoid of any real pressures. Neurotic anxiety is, in a deep sense, a fear of one's own drives and impulses, a fear of losing control over the beast inside one.

The causes of neurotic anxiety are complex, but basically they boil down to the fact that the child is not helped by those around him to recognise and come to terms with his instincts. Throughout life, there is a part of him that remains a stranger to the rest of him, and he lives a kind of Jekyll and Hyde existence, forever on the brink of self-made catastrophe. Should he give way to his id, we get what Freud called *the acting-out of impulses*, as when an apparently docile and well controlled child has a fearsome outburst of rage, or a respectable middle-aged lady goes on a shop-lifting spree. Far from helping the person concerned, acting out of impulses usually makes things much worse. He confesses afterwards to not knowing what came over him, and in the future goes in dread lest the same thing should happen again.

Realistic anxiety   Realistic anxiety occurs when the ego dominates, though what happens here is not that the ego itself poses a threat, but that it is faced with so many real difficulties and terrors in the external world that it requires an undue share of psychic energy to deal with them. The person beset with realistic anxiety has little energy left to enjoy the pleasures of the id (e.g. in extreme cases he may be unable to eat or to show a normal sex drive) or to devote to super-ego demands such as the welfare of others.

Extra-strong examples of realistic anxiety were termed by Freud *traumas*, and usually take the form of brutal emotional shocks or frightening experiences, but realistic anxiety is also caused in children by such things as excessive demands for academic success or standards of behaviour, by a background of domestic strife, or even by the uncertainties of having to start a new school or work with a new teacher.

Moral anxiety   If the super-ego dominates, we get what Freud called moral anxiety, an anxiety in which the individual is trapped in an over-rigid value system taken over from his parents. If it is the *ego-ideal* side of the super-ego that dominates, the individual is excessively high-minded and perfectionist, prompted by lofty ideals which have more to do with an unrealistic 'virtue' than with truth and compassion. If it is the *conscience* that dominates, he is compulsively on guard against anything that might arouse feelings of guilt, and he rejects both the pleasure principle of the id and the reality principle of the ego and inhabits instead an unreal world of taboos and forbidden things.

Both in children and in adults, guilt feelings in the person who suffers from moral anxiety can be so threatening that, whenever he has done something which he conceives as wrong, he will actively seek punishment in order to reduce them. Where punishment is not forthcoming, he will often torture himself with feelings of unworthiness and inadequacy, sometimes developing ritualistic gestures such as excessive (*obsessional–compulsive*) handwashing in order symbolically to rid himself of them.

Ego-defence mechanisms

Although these three forms of anxiety stem from different systems within the personality, it is possible for the same person to experience all three of them at once. But, whether he experiences one or all three, it is always the ego that does the experiencing. The id and the super-ego can cause anxiety, but they never suffer it themselves. It is the ego, with its conscious processes, that is the battlefield upon which the personality fights out its civil war. And, whenever the ego is weakened by one of the three forms of anxiety, it has less psychic energy left to fight a possible battle against one of the other two. Thus, to take up again our example of the normally well-controlled child who suddenly surprises us all with his temper tantrum, it may be that he has recently suffered a bout of realistic anxiety, such as the break-up of his parents' marriage, which draws off so much of his psychic energy that he is unable to maintain his customary defence against his ever-present neurotic anxiety. The id breaks through these defences, and the child behaves in what seems an utterly uncharacteristic way.

It is fair to point out at this juncture that, in all three forms of anxiety, there may be no obvious symptoms to the onlooker right up until the moment of breakdown. The individual may control his anxiety so well that it not until the ego is suddenly overwhelmed by having to fight a battle on yet another front that we get any idea of the pressures he has been under. But of course, the better we know people, the more sensitive we should be to these things.

Freud considered that the ego possesses certain weapons which it can use in its fight to retain control over the personality. These weapons he termed *ego-defence mechanisms*. We all of us unwittingly develop them to some extent in childhood, but they require a great amount of psychic energy to maintain, and normally as we grow older we develop more rational ways of coping with ourselves. Where we fail to do so, we tie up so much energy in ego defence mechanisms that little is left for more productive activity. Chief amongst these mechanisms are the following.

Repression   The ego tries to blot out the cause of the anxiety, to put it out of the conscious mind altogether. Repression is one of the commonest defence mechanisms, but its short-coming is that repressed material is not really forgotten at all, but merely sinks down into the id, serving to charge the latter more fully with energy than ever, making neurotic anxiety even more likely. The example of the child losing his temper that we gave above would be an instance of repressed material, in this case aggression, suddenly flooding back to take control of conscious behaviour. Repression can also come back in disguised form, as when a child's repressed hatred of a sibling shows itself in antagonism towards the things at which the other excels.

Projection   The ego attributes to other people those urges – and failings – which it is fearful of recognising in itself. Thus the child who is hostile to others escapes this hostility by claiming it is the other children who are always against him; or the person who is afraid of speaking out avoids admitting it by constantly haranguing others for their silence.

Rationalisation   The ego advances an apparently reasonable argument to explain away something that it finds too painful if explained truthfully. Thus a sadistic adult may rationalise his use of corporal punishment by insisting it is for the good of the child.

Reaction formation   The ego defends against one of the id's disturbing urges by placing an intense emphasis upon its opposite. Reaction formation is used particularly when this urge outrages the super-ego, thus causing moral anxiety. The child, for example, who feels hatred for his parents may become an excessively dutiful and apparently loving son. Or the person who has a strong sex drive may become an anti-pornography campaigner. Reaction formation is always distinguishable from genuine emotion by the fact that it is *exaggerated*.

Regression   The ego regresses to a form of behaviour that was successful in gaining attention and sympathy, and thus in lowering anxiety, in the past. Thus a child who feels threatened by the arrival of a new baby may revert to babyish behaviour himself, or a child who is unhappy in a new school may revert to tearful, overdependent behaviour at home.

Compensation   For one of the id's drives that cannot be satisfied, the ego substitutes one that can. The adolescent, for example, who fails to attract the opposite sex, may compensate by overeating. Closely allied to compensation is *sublimation*, when the ego directs frustrated energy into higher cultural goals (Freud saw much artistic activity as examples of sublimation).

Various other ego-defence mechanisms have been recognised as important since the time of Freud, many of them readily recognisable to the teacher. We have already looked at one of these in chapter 2, when we said that a child who is unsuccessful in school may protect his self-esteem (which is part of the ego) by rejecting the standards that the school sets. Another child may protect self-esteem by withdrawing from anything that has to do with competition, or may make the excuse of imagined illness.

(Hypochondria, as this process is called, may also be an example of attention-seeking behaviour in a child who feels himself neglected). Another form of defence may be excessive cynicism, or a hypercritical attitude towards the efforts of others.

Normal development

From what has been said already, it should be clear that Freud saw normal development as taking place when the id, the ego, and the super-ego are in a state of balance, and when the ego-defence mechanisms are being steadily replaced by more mature and efficient ways of dealing with one's problems. As normal development progresses, the individual also outgrows excessive dependence upon the primitive primary processes of the id, and learns to displace the energy associated with these processes into the socially acceptable secondary processes of the ego. This *displacement*, according to Freud, explains all the interests, attitudes and aspirations of the mature personality. Through orderly displacement, the id's drives are channelled into developmental stages such as those proposed by Erikson (chapter 2), aggressive drives becoming, for example, autonomy, determination, and leadership, while self-preservation drives become industry and competence, and the libido drive becomes marriage and parenthood.

One of the best known, and most controversial, aspects of Freudian theory is that this normal development proceeds through a number of what are called psychosexual stages, during each of which the instinctive drives that have to be displaced and socialised are centred on a separate erogenous zone of the body, and the individual is therefore maximally sensitive to experiences associated with it (the so-called oral, anal and genital phases). Perhaps because of its frank treatment of the sex drive, this part of Freud's work always attracts great interest, but it is of doubtful relevance to education. Few psychologists would accept it as a very accurate picture of what really happens to the personality during the years concerned. However, we can derive certain broad generalisations from it, which, taken together with the rest of Freud's work, suggest the sort of things that we must bear in mind as adults if we want to help children avoid the excessive forms of anxiety examined above.

Basically, it seems that we should take care not to set the child at war with himself. We set him at war by making him reject the drives of the id, particularly its extra-strong drives such as sex and aggression. These drives are present in children from birth onwards, and the child should be helped to recognise them, accept them, and gradually learn to channel their energy into socially acceptable forms. We also set him at war by endowing him with an overdeveloped super-ego, which demands impossible things of him, or fills him with guilt about the drives of his id. The super-ego should contain only necessary moral and social restraints, and by explaining these to the child at the time they are enforced we help him keep them within the range of his conscious thinking, so that he can subject them to rational debate as he grows older (much as we said in chapter 2 that the adolescent should be encouraged to talk and think things through).

Freud tells us that many of the things that we make the child reject or repress are not bad in themselves, but simply make us as adults feel uncomfortable, usually because we were not allowed to come to terms with them in our own childhood. It is not easy for us to accept that the child may at times feel intense hatred for a parent or a teacher, or that he may have strong sexual desires, or that he may want to run away rather than to stay and face a threatening situation, but all these things are natural responses. A child should not be made to feel guilty because of these feelings. Instead he should be encouraged to bring them into the open, to discuss them and confront them. Only by a frank recognition of their existence can the child be helped to control them, and to integrate them into his developing personality. If he is forced to repress them, they will remain fermenting in the id, denying him a source of creative energy, forcing him to erect rigid defence mechanisms, and awaiting their chance to burst back into consciousness and overwhelm him.

Criticisms of Freud

We have devoted a fair amount of space to Freud because of the great attention his work has attracted over the years, both outside and within education. In addition he provides us with a vocabulary in which to discuss personality theory, since, as we have suggested, many of his terms are now part and parcel of the language of psychology.

But there is another reason for spending time on Freud. It is unlikely that any man would have had the impact that he has had upon Western thought unless there were recognisable truths in some of what he says. In this chapter, I have tried to avoid most of Freud's more controversial ideas and present only those that seem to contain these truths.

This is not to say that all the points of Freudian theory that we have raised are based upon firm evidence. Like most innovative thinkers, Freud derived many of his ideas from intuition, and those ideas represent a groping towards a theory rather than a finished theory itself. There may not literally be an id, an ego and a super-ego, yet these three systems provide us with a model for discussing the personality, for seeing how heredity and environment may interact, and for isolating the causes of personality breakdown. There may be many more ego-defence mechanisms, and they may operate differently from the ways suggested by Freud, but his suggestions help us to understand how people may protect themselves from anxiety, and how inappropriate and damaging many of their methods for doing so can be. There may not be three clearly defined kinds of anxiety, but Freud shows us some of the ways in which anxiety can be created, and the different effects it can have upon the individual concerned.

Freud himself never saw his theory as a complete one. He accepted that it would be changed and altered in the light of new evidence, and his own frequent tinkerings with it highlight this point. Many psychologists claim that this very flexibility is a weakness. They say that, because Freudian theory can be adjusted to accommodate virtually any new findings, it is impossible ever to prove or disprove it. Like a piece of putty, it can be moulded to take on the right shape to accommodate any criticisms that are levelled at it, and that hard experimental evidence in support of it is therefore lacking (Eysenck and Wilson 1973). This is true up to a point, but it fails to take account of the advances in our thinking that have stemmed from Freud. As we have indicated, he has stressed the importance of early childhood in personality development, the importance of the unconscious in our mental life and in influencing, unbeknown to us, much of our behaviour and motivation, and the fact that normal and abnormal behaviour are on a continuum, since all of us suffer from *some* anxiety, from *some* inappropriate defence mechanisms. Highly anxious people are just a little further along the continuum than are the majority of us.

In addition there have in recent years been a number of interesting experiments that seem to reveal the workings of unconscious processes, and the way in which such processes may sometimes prevent people from correctly perceiving or remembering material that is painful to them (see, for instance, Fonagy 1981). This could lend experimental support to the existence of Freud's unconscious defence mechanisms. Similarly, work with factor analysis lends at least some weight to Freud's conceptualisation of id, ego and super-ego, though it suggests they may need various modifications (see Kline 1983).

On the other side of the coin, Eysenck (most recently 1985) argues that, in addition to lacking much in the way of experimental support, Freudian theory has been actively harmful to psychology in that it has diverted us from a properly scientific investigation of the causes of personality problems, and has provided us with a technique (psychoanalysis) of doubtful value in treating these problems. Exploring the unconscious by means of free association and other Freudian techniques may be all very well, but in the long run there is little hard evidence that it actually does the patient much good.

In chapter 6 we shall look at the alternative methods of treatment for personality problems advocated by Eysenck, but we must leave the debate on the value of Freud's work to rumble on. For the present, the best conclusion is perhaps still that of Brown (1964): namely, that without knowing all the answers Freud at least knew the kinds of questions psychologists ought to be asking.

Other psychodynamic approaches

Two of the most eminent of Freud's followers were C. G. Jung (1875–1961) and Alfred Adler (1870–1937). Both introduced so much new thinking into psychology as to be worthy of far more space than I can devote to them here. From an educational point of view, the most important aspect of this thinking is that, although both men accepted the existence and the importance of man's basic, animalistic drives, they rejected Freud's notion that these drives are the only innate motivating force behind human behaviour. Eventually they both broke completely with Freud, and each started his own movement within psychodynamic psychology.

Jung, the more complex and mystical thinker of the two, and the founder of what is known as *analytical* psychology, saw man as motivated over and above his animalistic urges by a drive towards self-discovery. As he grows older, by studying himself and by plumbing his unconscious through an analysis of dreams, memories and thoughts, he can come to know more about himself, to understand better his own motivation, his aspirations, his strengths. Unlike Freud, Jung held that the personality is whole at birth, and only breaks down into conflicting systems in the face of adverse experiences. The search for self-discovery is therefore really a search for the wholeness with which we are born, and which in potential we carry with us throughout life. When we find this wholeness, we become what Jung called *individuated*, and he would have agreed that the individuated man has those qualities which we listed in chapter 2 as belonging to the mature personality.

From the educational point of view, one of Jung's most interesting concepts is that we can fail to find ourselves by being forced by environment, by parents, teachers and society generally, to create a *persona*, a kind of public mask that hides our true feelings from others and from ourselves. The mechanisms behind the persona are not dissimilar from those that Freud suggested are behind the super-ego, with the child being made to reject much of his true self and to assume the unrealistic code of social prohibitions and conventions of other people. Jung took a great interest in formal education, and saw teachers as of almost equal importance to parents in helping the child avoid an over-strong persona and develop towards individuation. The teacher can best provide this help, Jung argued, if she herself possesses the self-knowledge that goes with individuation, and can thus avoid inflicting any of her own problems upon the class. She should also encourage the child to bring unconscious thoughts to the surface, not only through allowing discussion but also by emphasising free expression in the arts and in the sciences, since this expression stems largely from the unconscious. And in every subject in the curriculum the teacher should encourage individuality. Each personality is unique, and can only achieve individuation in its own way. Where conformity and rules are essential, the child should be helped to see, much as we have already stressed, the purpose behind these rules, and the distinction between social convenience and moral imperative.

Jung also developed, though he did not originate, the idea that some people are *extroverted* in their personalities (that is, that they are oriented, probably innately, towards other people and towards the stimuli of the outside world), while others are *introverted* (that is, they are oriented more towards their own inner states of mind. These terms have been further developed by Eysenck, and are proving very influential in education. We shall be returning to them when we discuss the latter's work in chapter 6.

Though Adler, the founder of what became known as *individual* psychology, was not strongly at variance with Jung on most of these points, he laid particular stress upon the extroverted side of man. Man is motivated, he claimed, over and above his basic needs and his drive towards self-discovery, by *social* drives – that is, by the desire to go out and interact with other people. It is from other people that he receives the major experiences of his life, from other people that he learns how to understand and eventually to control himself. In common with Jung, Adler saw man as having much more to say in his own destiny than did Freud. Man has a *creative self*, a kind of innate ego, that helps him from an early stage to start making sense of the world, to seek out new experiences, and to create from them and from his self-knowledge a *lifestyle*, a characteristic and unique way of coping with the world that is constantly open to further development in the light of new findings.

Educationally, Adler's concept of lifestyle is an important one. A child's lifestyle determines how he reacts to the experiences that we offer him at school. The lifestyle contains *complexes* – that is, associations of ideas and feelings that he has about things – such as the *inferiority complex* (which Coopersmith's low self-esteem boys in chapter 2 certainly possessed). The inferiority complex means that the ideas and feelings that a child has about himself all contain the belief that he is less effective than are the people around him. This belief colours his whole approach to life. It affects his school work, his long-term goals, and even his interpretation of fairness, authority, and human relationships. Adler's followers have expanded the idea of complexes to cover all aspects of the lifestyle. We can, for example, talk about a child's negative complex about school, which means he rejects school, and may through this rejection come to despise everything to do with books or learning or the gaining of qualifications in life. He might also have a negative complex about sport, or women, or anything else. (Useful as the notion of complexes is, we need not pursue it further as it is somewhat similar to Kelly's theory of constructs, which we shall be discussing in chapter 4).

Adler saw the possession of an inferiority complex as indicating that the individual has failed to achieve the *superiority* that he held to be an essential part of the social urge. In the well-adjusted person, this superiority means power over oneself rather than over others, and the ability to use this power for social good. Anyone handicapped in the drive for superiority, by, for example, a physical or environmental disability, may compensate (Adler borrowed the term from Freud and further developed it) by trying extra hard, and may achieve spectacular success, as when the stammerer becomes a great orator or the weakly child a great athlete. But some kinds of compensation can be overdone, as when the socially deprived child develops into the political extremist, or the bullied child becomes the tyrannical boss.

After a period of relative eclipse, both Jung and Adler are tending once again to become influential as thinkers. They provide a useful counterbalance to Freud within psychodynamic psychology in that their picture of man is a broader, more optimistic one. Both saw man as having the power to change his personality even into old age, instead of being imprisoned in the experiences of childhood. And Jung stressed that man has creative, mystical depths, while Adler saw him as the seeker and instigator of social experiences and not as simply the victim of them.

Psychodynamic theories and personality testing

Psychodynamics plumbs the individual's personality mostly through the techniques of the consulting-room, such as free association, but it has given rise to a number of measuring devices which are used in general psychology. These are of interest to the teacher because the educational psychologist sometimes employs them when diagnosing personality problems in child guidance, and they also figure from time to time in educational research.

The best known of these tests are probably the *projective techniques* (see Semeonoff 1976) which operate on the assumption that people will project their conscious and often their unconscious personality problems (through the ego-defence mechanism of projection) into any interpretation which they are invited to give of an ambiguous stimulus. This is rather akin to what happens when we see faces in the fire or pictures in the clouds. The kind of faces and pictures that we see may owe as much to our unconscious preoccupations as to the shapes that are actually there. A timid, frightened person may tend to see threatening things; a girl who unconsciously longs to be married may see things to do with a wedding; a person with repressed aggression may see knives or guns.

The first projective technique to be developed was the Rorschach Inkblot Test (Herman Rorschach 1922). The test consists of ten symmetrical inkblots (rather like the 'butterflies' that children make by shaking paint on to a sheet of paper, folding it over and opening it out again), five in colour and five in black and white. The person being tested, who it is claimed can be as young as three years old, looks at each blot in turn and says what he thinks it looks like. His responses are scored in terms of such things as their content, their localisation (does he respond to the whole inkblot or only part of it?) and their determinants (does he respond mainly to colour or to form?) So involved is this scoring, and so complex is the analysis of what it means in personality terms, that it is claimed that it takes many months of specialist training before psychologists who want to use the test are competent to do so. Unfortunately, there is little evidence that this is time well spent. The test suffers from the lack of any real attempt at standardisation. That is, we have little idea how most normal people would respond to it, so we have little idea, either, of how far from normality a particular person's responses may actually be. And we have no consistent evidence on how much connection there is, if any, between these responses and how a person actually deals with a real-life problem. Although the Rorschach is still thought to be one of the most popular clinical tests of personality, particularly in the USA, it seems probable that these shortcomings, unless remedied, will mean a gradual fall from favour.

A more straightforward projective technique is the Thematic Apperception Test (TAT), devised by Henry Murray in 1943. It consists of a number of ambiguous black and white pictures, mainly of social situations, about each of which the person being tested is asked to tell a story. His responses are then analysed in terms of Murray's concepts of *need* and *press*, a need being a primary organic force (such as Freud's instincts or Adler's social drive), while a press is anything within the environment that helps or hinders the satisfaction of that need (for instance, a need for social approval can be aided by the press of a pretty face). The theory is that, in telling a story about each of the pictures in the test, the individual will attribute to the characters in the story his own needs and presses. He may suggest, for example, that a pensive man in one of the pictures is 'worrying about his failure at work', and suggest that this failure is owing to the fact that 'everyone is against him'.

The TAT has now been supplemented by extra pictures which are for use with children aged from eight to fourteen and for children even younger than this there is the Children's Apperception Test devised by Bellak and Bellak in 1955, which carries its own supplement of pictures designed to test for problems associated particularly with school. In all these tests, Murray's original marking-scheme has been added to, and there are now many alternative schemes available.

Another set of projective techniques utilises the notion that children project something of themselves into their drawings and their stories. The Goodenough Draw-a-Man-Test, revised in 1963 (Goodenough and Harris), and originally a test of intelligence, has been widely used in this context, and there are also tests specifically designed for the purpose, such as the Harms Test (1945). Yet other tests, such as the Lowenfeld World Test, are designed to allow the tester to watch children playing with dolls, and to see what roles they assign to them and how they make them interact with each other.

The bewildering abundance of projective techniques, of which the foregoing are only a small sample, must not be allowed to hide the fact that, like the Rorschach, they lack standardisation. In some cases, there is also disagreement on how they should be marked. Inevitably, this restricts their usefulness. We have no clear idea on how reliable or how valid they are, and some psychologists suggest that their most useful function is simply to get children to talk to the psychologist when they attend for child guidance. This is probably unfair. There seems little doubt that projective techniques can tell us something about personality, just as the teacher often feels she can learn about children from studying the themes that they habitually choose in their creative writing and in their free art work, the characters they create, the freedom or inhibition with which they use words, shapes and colours. These things give information on the children's interests, ambitions, and fears, and on the amount of flexibility or restraint with which they tackle life.

In any case, as Semeonoff (1981) points out, it is somewhat meaningless to expect from projective techniques the kind of 'validity' we demand in questionnaire tests such as those we discuss in chapter 5. Projective techniques are designed to assess the private world of the individual's *experience* rather than the public world of his *behaviour*, and as such they cannot be expected to show what we might term scientific precision. Until better methods are devised, it is sometimes a question either of using projective techniques or of accepting that this private world must remain inaccessible to the psychologist.

4

Humanistic Psychology and Personality

Humanistic models of personality share similarities with psychodynamic ones, and are also primarily idiographic in approach, but they differ from them importantly in that they insist man must be studied as a *person*, rather than simply as a collection of neuroses. They also differ from Freud, though not from Jung and Adler, in that they insist that personality is never complete. Throughout life, man is in a constant state of development, much as we saw that Erikson holds him to be. Far from having his personality fixed in the first five or six years of life, he is in a constant state of *becoming something else* (it is this belief which has led some humanistic theories to attract to themselves the title of 'existential psychology').

We have already met one humanistic psychologist, Gordon Allport, whose work we looked at in our discussion of the mature personality in chapter 2. In many senses, Erikson could also be put in this category. But the person with whom we shall start our discussion is Abraham Maslow (1908–70), who is taken by many to have established humanistic psychology as a significant force with his foundation in 1962 of the American Association for Humanistic Psychology. From this date to the present, humanistic psychology has seen a rapid growth in its support, and its influence upon educational thinking in the USA has been considerable.

What such people as Maslow mean when they say that man must be studied as a person is that man is clearly motivated by a whole range of things over and above the instinctive needs proposed by Freud, or even the need for self-discovery or social relationships (Jung and Adler). Maslow criticises the dynamic psychologists for missing the essential diversity of man. Of course man is motivated by the needs which they propose, but it is wrong to lump all men together and say that everyone has sex, or self-discovery, or social relationships, or what not, as his *overriding* need. All men are different, and psychological theory must take account of this fact.

So what Maslow proposes is that the psychologist can do no more than suggest a general framework of needs or motivation, within which each personality will find its own niche. And such a framework, Maslow argues, must take account of the fact that history shows man is motivated not just by his own pleasure, his own desire for self-discovery, his own need to establish himself socially, but also by all kinds of ideals, by self-sacrifice, by the arts, by the urge towards scientific discovery. The framework which he proposes (1970) is therefore in the form of a hierarchy. Once the earlier, more basic needs such as those of the Freudian instincts are satisfied, man frees himself to develop his higher-order needs, and it is these that set him above the level of the animals. The hierarchy, working from the basic needs upwards, is

1   physiological needs (e.g. food, sex, shelter);
2   safety needs (e.g. protection from neglect);
3   social needs (e.g. social acceptance);
4   ego needs (e.g. self-esteem, status);
5   self-fulfilment needs (e.g. creativity, insight).

This model fits in well with Erikson's developmental stages (chapter 3). Through the satisfaction of needs 1 and 2 the child learns trust, through 3 and 4 he learns competence and identity, and through 5 he learns generativity and self-acceptance. Maslow argues that often the reason why deprived children make less progress educationally than they should (and, indeed, why poorer countries make less progress than do wealthy ones) is that failure to satisfy basic physiological needs prevents the individual from developing the higher-order needs (3 onwards in the hierarchy) which lie behind educational motivation and artistic and scientific discovery. Maslow calls these needs *meta needs* to distinguish them from the basic ones, and insisted that, although numbers 3 and 5 in the hierarchy include the needs proposed by Adler and Jung respectively, they include much more besides. The individual who successfully satisfies the needs at the top of the hierarchy achieves what Maslow calls *self-actualisation*, and many of the characteristics that we listed for the mature personality in chapter 2 were assembled by Allport from what Maslow has to say about the self-actualised person.

Maslow's theory is an interesting one, but the trouble is that it does not tell us much about how meta needs actually develop, or how we can go about measuring them. Many people see this as no problem, and are content to leave matters where Maslow has left them, but psychologists need to measure things. Perhaps, indeed, this is one of their own meta needs. They also like to explain why things happen. Why should one person want to spend his life fishing while another wants to split the atom? Why, to put it somewhat more prosaically, should one person prefer to go out to parties while another would much rather stay in with a good book? And, through her own interest in children, the teacher usually shares the psychologist's concern with things of this order. We can turn to another humanistic psychologist, Carl Rogers, to find out a little more about them.

Carl Rogers

Rogers (b. 1902), like the psychodynamic psychologists, has gained much of his experience from clinical work. Besides his influence within this field and within education, he has also had a marked impact upon the fields of counselling, business studies and social work. His ideas are not easy to summarise in a few pages, and the interested reader is strongly advised to turn to Rogers's own work for further elaboration (e.g. 1961, 1974).

Rogers is sometimes called a *phenomenologist*, because he places emphasis not upon what actually happens in the individual's environment, but upon what the individual *thinks* is happening. In childhood, in particular, the individual often gets an impression of what is going on that is quite different from that of other people. We only have to listen to the conflicting accounts that two sincere witnesses give of the same event to be convinced of this fact. Rogers is thus emphasising not only that personality is unique, but also that each of us inhabits a unique world, a world of subjective experiences known only to ourselves. Certainly we can *tell* other people about these experiences, but, although they may nod their heads, there is no knowing that they understand them in quite the way that we do.

Rogers calls this subjective world that we each inhabit our *phenomenal field*. Like Freud, he accepts that this field contains conscious and unconscious factors. The conscious mind deals mainly with experiences that can be symbolised (that is, put into language, talked about, understood) while the unconscious deals with those that cannot (for instance, irrational fears and desires). The primary threat to personality, as Rogers sees it, is that sometimes the individual symbolises conscious experiences incorrectly – that is, he makes sense of them in the wrong way. This would happen if, for example, a child interprets the teacher's attempt to help him as a sign that she is censuring him. It would also happen if he misunderstands a number concept. As a result of incorrect symbolisation, the individual behaves inappropriately in the future (in our example, he might stop consulting the teacher, or he might mishandle the next step in number learning). Sometimes these incorrect symbolisations are put right; sometimes they persist. Where the individual possesses a large number of incorrect symbolisations, Rogers says that he is out of *congruence* – that is, that his phenomenal field does not really approximate to the real world outside.

Although accepting Freud's emphasis on the divide between conscious and unconscious experience, Rogers has not adopted his model of the id, ego and super-ego. Instead, he talks of the *organism*, which is the total man, basic and meta needs, conscious and unconscious and all, and the *self*, which is that part of the organism that contains all the ideas we have about ourselves – all the things, in fact, that we feel define each of us as a unique individual. The self also contains the *ideal self*, which as in Freudian theory is our picture of the kind of person we should like to become. Unlike Freud though, Rogers sees the ideal self as learnt not just from our parents, but as created by our own meta needs, and by our own aspirations.

Just as there should be congruence between the phenomenal field and the real world, so Rogers insists that there must be congruence between the organism and the self, and between the self and the ideal self. An example will show how this works. Suppose in some imaginary world it were possible to let children do exactly as they liked all the time, and indeed to praise them lavishly for doing so. Such children, however else they might grow up, would certainly not grow up incongruent in any way. Their picture of the world as being a place in which they can do as they like (i.e. their phenomenal fields), their own desire to do as they like (i.e. their organisms), their picture of themselves as children who always do as they like (i.e. their selves), and their picture of themselves as children who ought to do as they like (i.e. their ideal selves) would all be completely in harmony, and therefore in congruence, with each other.

However, regrettably or otherwise, the world is not the sort of place in which we can do as we like all the time. Thus, inevitably, we all develop some incongruence during our lives. We have to avoid physical dangers, however enticing, we have to study the wishes and the rights of others. The child who wants to obey the dictates of his organism and assert his will over another has to be stopped. The child who demands the constant attention of his parents has to learn that they, too, have lives of their own to lead.

It is, indeed, Rogers's ideas on how we can best help the child to learn to live with some degree of incongruence that contain his main contribution to educational thinking. Rogers agrees with Freud that the young baby is selfish, but he attributes this not so much to the basic drives of the id as to the simple fact that the child inhabits his own phenomenal field. He does not know (how can he?) that other people have different phenomenal fields from his own, and are therefore not there just for his benefit. He has to *learn* about the phenomenal fields of others. The way to get him to do this, Rogers argues, is not to make him feel guilty for being what he is, but to get him to empathise with others – that is, to put himself in their shoes and imagine how he would feel if he were they. Thus the child who wants to bully another child should not be labelled evil for it, which may only lead to excessive incongruence between his organism (which perhaps genuinely wants to assert itself at school to make up for the bullying it receives at home) and his self (which, if it wants to avoid the label 'evil', now has to convince itself it does not really want to bully after all). Instead, he should be reminded that within his own phenomenal field he has a dislike of being bullied, and that other children have the same kind of dislike. Other children, in fact, feel pain and fear and so on just as much as he does.

This, of course, makes considerable demands upon the teacher. It is much easier to call a child naughty than to explain to him the feelings of others. But, as we saw in chapter 2 when discussing self-esteem, labels such as 'naughty' or 'evil' become incorporated by the child into his picture of himself. If he collects too many of these labels, Rogers argues, he begins to see the wishes of his organism as a constant threat, particularly if he has a well-developed ideal self, and may defend against them by a series of ego-defence mechanisms which Rogers agrees are very much the ones defined by Freud. The incongruent person, the person at odds with himself, tends to be tense and anxious, afraid of losing control, defensive and often rigid in his thinking, and unable to discover his true identity. Ultimately, he is in danger of losing all touch with reality, and, should the repressed wishes of his organism break through into consciousness, he may lose all sense of self and suffer a complete personality breakdown.

The congruent person, on the other hand, is able to develop (i.e. to actualise himself) along the lines laid down for him by inheritance. He becomes, in other words, the person his inheritance 'intended' him to be. Freed from internal conflict, he is able to turn his attentions outwards, to empathise with other people, to enjoy art and beauty, to interest himself in science. Through this broadening of the personality he comes to experience the satisfaction to be gained from serving and helping others, from creating things, from improving the quality of life generally. Because he inhabits his own phenomenal field, with his own unique genetic endowment, the way in which he does all these things, the way in which he acquires and expresses interests, will be unique to himself.

In addition to helping the child to understand and empathise with others, it is essential to his development of congruence that we show the same empathy to him. This is all part and parcel of the child's need for the *positive regard* of the adults in his life, for their love and approval. Rogers claims this is one of the strongest needs that he has found in the organism. (Significantly, it does not appear at all amongst Freud's major instincts.) It is this need that makes the child obey teachers and parents, even when this obedience means forgoing other organismic wishes. Much of the child's self, and of his ideal self, is formed in response to the need to gain and to keep this positive regard. Where the regard is only given to him conditionally, and there is the constant threat of its being withdrawn as a punishment for bad behaviour, the child will sacrifice more and more of his organismic wishes in order to retain it, and thus will become more and more incongruent. This point was referred to in the discussion of self-esteem in chapter 2. No child is likely to experience satisfactory personality development if he goes in constant fear that the adults in his life are ready to turn their positive feelings for him on and off like a tap.

Rogers's insistence upon this point, and upon the uniqueness of each person's phenomenal field, is evident in the techniques of psychotherapy and of counselling that he has developed. Psychotherapy (the treatment of people with extreme personality problems) belongs, like psychoanalytical techniques, to clinical psychology, but counselling is used widely within education, both by the educational psychologist working through the child-guidance service, and at a non-specialist level by teachers themselves. Rogers's methods of counselling are known as *client-centred* (see, for example, Rogers 1957), because the emphasis is upon the client working out the solutions to his own problems, in the atmosphere of positive regard and empathic understanding that the counsellor offers him, rather than upon the counsellor acting as an authority figure and telling the client what he should and should not do. Because each client is unique, there can be no ready-made formula to offer him, as sometimes happens in the forms of counselling that have derived from psychoanalytical theories. The fact that the counsellor is prepared to listen to the client, to accept him for what he is, to prompt him gently when he has difficulties in expressing himself, to approve of his attempts at dealing with his problems, to show understanding (though not weakness) over his incongruences and to be generally non-judgemental and encouraging, is what counts, says Rogers. And the warmth and friendliness of the Rogerian therapist and counsellor is often in marked contrast to the more remote, objective approach of the Freudian.

Even in the most hardened child, Rogers claims, the need for positive regard is still there. The experienced teacher can usually spot the form this need takes, and use it sympathetically to increase the child's socialisation and academic motivation. However, Rogers has shown that a technique called Q-sorting, originally introduced by Stevenson in 1953, is a useful adjunct in exploring this and other aspects of the child's phenomenal field.

In Q-sorting, we prepare a number of cards, each with a self-descriptive statement such as 'I work hard', 'I am popular', and we ask the child to sort them into a number of piles, ranging from a pile which contains the descriptions that are 'most like me' down to the pile which contains those that are 'least like me'. The number of cards which a child can place in any one pile is usually restricted, so that we get a fair spread across the piles (often a normal distribution is used, with most cards in the middle piles, tapering off to least cards in the two extremes). The number of cards is not critical, but for secondary-school children twenty-five to fifty cards, and five to seven piles, is about right.

Q-sorting gives us a useful picture of how the child views himself, and of course we can repeat the process, using different cards, for any part of his phenomenal field that we wish to explore (e.g. 'my work', 'my ideal person').

Another, even more versatile, test is Osgood's Semantic Differential (Osgood et al. 1957). When employing the test, we write a concept at the head of a sheet of paper (e.g. 'the person I am'), and then list below it adjectives that might define this concept, together with their opposites:

strong ——: ——: ——: ——: ——: ——: ——: weak
sad ——: ——: ——: ——: ——: ——: ——: happy
honest ——: ——: ——: ——: ——: ——: ——: dishonest
cruel ——: ——: ——: ——: ——: ——: ——: kind
active ——: ——: ——: ——: ——: ——: ——: passive

The child is asked to rate himself on the seven-point scale for each adjective. For example, if he thinks he scores full marks for 'strong' he will put a cross nearest to 'strong' and furthest from 'weak'. At the end of the exercise, we have a useful profile of the child's self-concept. We could then ask him to repeat the process, but this time rating not himself but 'the person I would like to be', and we could look for correlations between the two profiles to examine how much congruence there is between the child's self and ideal self. Or we could rate the child ourselves or ask someone else to rate him, and thus see how much congruence there is between another person's picture of the child and his own view. As with Q-sorting, the Semantic Differential can be used to explore any aspect of the child's phenomenal field.

Criticisms of humanistic psychology

Nothing is more confusing than a book that constantly describes theories only a few pages later to knock them down again. Unfortunately, in such a field as personality, with all its perplexities and imponderables, a certain amount of knocking-down is unavoidable if we hope to present our subject as honestly as we can. So, as with Freud and psychoanalysis, we have to make some reference to the weaknesses of humanistic psychology before we leave it.

The most obvious criticism is that none of the measuring-techniques that humanistic psychologists use really takes account of unconscious factors. And of course techniques such as Q-sorting allow the child to give us dishonest responses if he so wishes. At other times he may be honest enough, but just not able to make fine-enough distinctions between the people or the events with which we are confronting him. Another criticism is that we have insufficient evidence on the reliability and validity of these techniques.

Turning to humanistic theories in general, they certainly present a much more optimistic picture of man than do psychoanalytical ones, but is this picture necessarily true? It is sometimes suggested that writers such as Maslow seem to be providing us more with an exercise in moral uplift than with an exercise in psychology. This is probably inaccurate, but the problem with concepts such as Maslow's meta needs is that they are so confoundedly difficult to demonstrate in practice. We know that man has an inbuilt need to seek food, and that he will go to great lengths to satisfy it, but it is much harder to demonstrate that he has an inbuilt, as opposed to a purely acquired, need to seek for self-fulfilment and for the deeper meaning of life. Nevertheless, recent research into humanistic theories as summarised for example by Smith (1981) indicates that even difficult areas such as self-actualisation can be subjected to research investigation. Both here and in terms of Rogers's theory of the self, such research has tended to support the ideas concerned and the various practical techniques derived from them.

The phenomenological approach of Rogers nevertheless attracts another criticism, which is that, if we each inhabit a *subjective* world, no one can really know what the *objective* world is like, and it thus becomes nonsense to talk about whether the child's constructs approximate to it or not. This is the kind of problem that philosophers love to argue about, and perhaps we had better leave them to get on with it. Common sense tells us that there appears to be some sort of consensus amongst us as to what everyday reality seems to be about, and the teacher has to get on with the job of helping children to cope with this reality. On balance, the humanistic approach seems to be one of the most useful ways the teacher has of thinking about children, and of studying each child's individual differences within the framework of the whole personality.

The final criticism that is levelled at humanistic psychologists, and one that leads us on neatly to chapter 5, is that they neglect the social context in which much of human behaviour takes place, and which seems highly instrumental in helping shape behaviour. True, they lay great stress on the importance of the child's relationships with adults, and, as we shall see shortly, Rogers has advanced numerous ideas on how groups of people can help each other tackle their individual problems through the open communication of feelings and ideas. But humanistic psychologists as a whole often seem to take insufficient account of the fact that both an individual's psychological conflicts on the one hand, and many of his short- and long-term goals on the other, can be caused on occasions less through such things as personal inadequacies or ambitions than through the daily pressures that come from working with other people. It may be, as well, that these pressures make personality less consistent than the humanistic psychologists assume it to be, that even people with mature personalities change more from day to day than these psychologists suggest.

For this reason, we shall now look at what are called *field theories* of personality. Like humanistic theories, their emphasis is upon the individual, but they place the individual within a social field, a field which contains forces and pressures that pull him first one way and then the other. They are of particular value to the teacher, since she spends much of her time dealing with children within the context of the classroom group.

5

Field and Social Models of Personality

Field models are similar to humanistic models in that they take account of the whole person, but differ in maintaining that variations between people in personality are occasioned less by inner processes than by the individual's psychological or life 'space' – that is, the context, primarily social, within which he lives his life. The best-known and most consistent field theory is that advanced by Kurt Lewin (1880–1945), and it has proved very influential within social psychology. Lewin's theory is represented diagramatically by three ellipses, one inside the other (figure 1). The innermost ellipse and the second ellipse represent the *person* (P), with the former being his inner world of thoughts and fantasies, and the latter the perceptual and motor faculties with which he makes contact with his external environment. The outer ellipse represents the immediate aspects of this environment (his *psychological environment*, or E), while all the space outside this represents the *foreign hull*, the rest of the individual's environment, which is too remote to touch him much as a person. Together, the three circles are his *life space*, the psychological limits of his immediate existence. Within this life space, the personality is formed, but Lewin rejected the notion of personality as a constant entity, or as necessarily following a set developmental path. As a result of the dynamic forces at work within the life field, the individual is subject to constant change, both influencing and being influenced by his environment at all times.

Lewin elaborated his theory to deal with the actual mechanics of how P becomes modified and developed in response to the events that take place in E, but for our purposes this adds little of practical value to the insights into such matters that we have already gained from the psychoanalysts and from humanistic psychology. What concerns us is the interaction between P and E, and to understand this we must first look at how E is structured.

Lewin (1935) saw E as divided ('differentiated') into a number of regions, each of which has relatively greater or lesser influence upon the individual. Early in life, these regions are few, consisting of the family and the immediate home environment, but, as the child grows older, new ones are added. He starts school, he makes friends, he joins things, his world becomes more complex. Each of these regions has boundaries between it and the others. School is a different social environment from home; home is different from the Brownies, or the Cubs, or the youth club, and so on. Where the boundaries between regions are low, the regions are said to be in *communication*, and the individual can move easily through his life space, or, as Lewin puts it, he can experience *locomotion*. School and home have the same values; he meets his school friends at the Cubs; he can be the same kind of person in each of the different social contexts of his life.

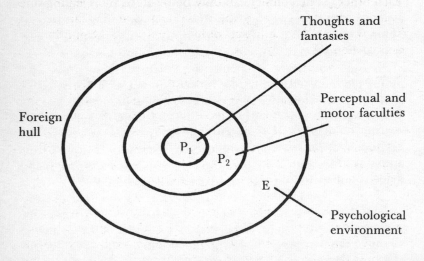

Figure 1

This locomotion can be of several different kinds: for example, it can be social (he can mix with different groups of people), vocational (as an adult he can change jobs), or intellectual (he can solve problems and thus tackle new areas of competence). A *valence* is the degree of importance that the individual attaches to a region (positive if the region is useful, negative if it is harmful), and a *vector* is the force that makes him want to move into, or out of, a region. The stronger the valence, positive or negative, the stronger the corresponding vector, positive or negative (for example, we all have a strong positive valence to move into employment if we are job-hunting, and at all times we have a negative valence to keep out of prison).

Psychological problems within P, such as Erikson's 'search for identity' (chapter 2) stem largely from the individual's inability to locomote easily between the regions in E, and particularly from conflicts which arise between these regions. These conflicts are of three main types.

Type one occurs when the individual is confronted by two positive valences of equal force, but the barrier dividing them is too high (as, for example, when his home and his school teach him value systems that directly conflict with each other). The conflict can only be resolved by rejecting one valence altogether, or by the individual changing himself in some way (e.g. the child acts differently at school from how he acts at home).

Type two occurs when the individual is confronted by two negative valences of equal force. For example, if a child works hard at a subject, he gets moved into a higher set, but with a teacher he dislikes. If he doesn't work hard, he stays in a lower set, but gets bored. If he cannot change one of these valences into a positive one (e.g. get to like the teacher) he may have to reject both of them (e.g. drop the subject altogether).

Type three occurs when the individual is confronted by positive and negative valences of equal force. For example, the child wants to move into the positive valence of having passed an exam, but can only do so by first moving into the negative valence of giving up his social life to prepare for the exam.

The school can help the child with these conflicts in two ways. First, it can avoid setting up any additional conflicts of its own (we discussed this when talking about adolescence in chapter 2), and, second, it can help him to make informed choices between the elements that make up the conflict (for instance, what will happen if the child gives up the subject, or if he doesn't pass the exam?). It is also in the nature of education itself to help a child to move freely between the important regions in his life. It widens his horizons, it equips him with intellectual competence and vocational skills, it teaches him verbal communication and some of the social skills. This is really what we mean when we talk about education's power to confer greater freedom upon people.

Research shows that many people resolve conflicts simply by conforming to the values of the region in which they happen to find themselves at any one time. A classic piece of research by Hartshorne and May back in 1928 showed that children are particularly prone to do this kind of thing, varying their interpretation of such values as honesty dependent upon whether the context of their behaviour involves teachers or other children. More recently, research has been directed towards identifying the personal qualities of people who succumb most readily to group pressures in this way. We saw in chapter 2 that children who are low in self-esteem seem more anxious for social approval, and therefore are more likely to succumb to such pressures, than are children who are high in self-esteem. Other research shows that authoritarian individuals tend to be conformers too, as do those who are submissive and those who are dependent.

One of the most interesting series of experiments into conformity was that carried out some years ago by Asch (1955). Asch asked groups of students to tackle a simple perceptual experiment that involved comparing the relative lengths of three straight lines. Before the experiment, all save one student in each group was secretly briefed to give the wrong answer, and attention was then focused upon the non-briefed students to see what their reactions would be. Although the error involved in the wrong answer was abundantly clear, no less than 37 per cent of the non-briefed students agreed with the rest of their groups rather than take on the role of odd man out. Subsequent experiments by Cruchfield (1955) showed that these conformers tended to be defensive, rigid and moralistic in personality, and intolerant of ambiguity (i.e. they always had to have everything cut and dried, in itself a sign of insecurity), while those who refused to conform tended to be independent, open, confident and secure.

More recently Milgram (1974) has produced experimental evidence to show the lengths to which conformist people will go in inflicting pain upon a third person when they are told to do so by the prestigious figure of the experimenter. Some conformers, whilst obviously experiencing reluctance and inner conflict, were even prepared to proceed beyond the point at which they were apparently inflicting severe physical damage.

It must be stressed, though, that, in experiments such as those of Asch and of Milgram, conformity to the group or to authority meant saying and doing things that were patently wrong. Sometimes when a group or those in authority are equally patently right, or when decisions have been arrived at democratically, it is equally a sign of personality problems to refuse to conform. To be the odd man out in such circumstances, particularly if as a result one holds up some important course of action, can be a sign of attention-seeking behaviour and of a bid for bogus significance. One becomes the centre of the discussion, one features prominently in people's thoughts, one basks in one's own cussedness.

Besides his interest in the individual within the group, Lewin was also very interested in the group itself. The whole subject of *group dynamics*, in fact, stems largely from his work. In group dynamics, the group (in our case the school or the class) can be thought of as an enlarged version of the psychological environment, E, defined above – that is, as an ever-changing field in which each individual group member represents a region. Some regions have stronger positive or negative valences than others (i.e. some children are particularly co-operative, or popular, or disruptive), and individual children are pushed and pulled by various vectors either towards or away from the regions around them. The group thus builds up tensions and conflicts, such as sub-group rivalries and hostilities. It also builds up group norms, hierarchies and pecking-orders. It develops group fads that come and go. And, of course, the popularity of individual teachers with the group can wax and wane.

Attempts by Lewin and others to find out which qualities of personality mark people out from the rest of their group as stars (extra-popular) or as leaders suggest that these qualities vary from group to group. A person who is successful in one group may be relatively ignored when he joins another. Stars, however, tend to be above average in intelligence and in confidence for their particular group, and Kelvin (1970) suggests that most leaders have the ability in some way to define the group (i.e. to give it direction, identity and standards), and to act as a source of rewards for group members (for instance, by conferring approval or status).

When it comes to leaders whose authority is imposed upon the group from outside (as in the case of teachers), Lewin (1942) found that the best way to get group co-operation is to allow the group some say in the setting of its own standards and work targets. Once these have been democratically accepted, there is considerable pressure by the group upon each of its members to conform to them. In an earlier, very well known experiment, Lewin, Lippitt and White (1939) found that, whereas adolescent boys produced their best work in such a democratic group, they became lost and confused in a *laissez-faire* group (i.e. one with no real adult direction), and rigid and conformist, with a tendency to kick over the traces when control was removed, in an authoritarian group with an autocratic adult leader (see also White and Lippitt 1960). It seems that, by a careful exercise of group democracy, the teacher can prompt children to show much more concern and responsibility for their own performance and for that of other group members. It becomes the job of everyone to help the child who has particular problems over his work or his behaviour, and often results are achieved which the teacher, left to struggle unaided, could never hope for.

Lewin and group therapy

Over the last two decades a whole new movement has grown up around the ideas of Lewin and of the humanistic psychologists, such as Rogers, in which a group of people rather than an individual analyst or therapist is used to help people to come to terms with their personality problems. Operating under a variety of titles such as 'T groups', 'encounter groups', 'sensitivity groups', these groups are usually run on democratic lines and aim, through the frank interchange of their members' feelings towards each other, and through an open discussion of each person's individual problems, to break down the barriers which separate people from one another. As these barriers are broken down, and as each group member begins to feel the support and the sympathy of the group, so is he encouraged to probe deeper and deeper into himself, and to bring to the surface those sentiments of inadequacy, of guilt, of rejection, that have lain hidden in the conscious and unconscious mind.

Under a trained leader, who remains carefully unobtrusive, but who monitors proceedings and acts skilfully to protect the more vulnerable group members from a too-abrupt assault on their defence mechanisms by the rest of the group, group therapy is now used extensively and to good effect in the rehabilitation of the mentally ill, of delinquents, of social casualties such as alcoholics, and also of those with extreme anxiety or low self-confidence. It is also used as a method in the training of personnel officers and managers in industry, and of social workers and others involved in the field of human relationships.

So far, group methods of this kind have not been widely used in teacher education or in schools themselves, but amateur groups of one sort and another have mushroomed amongst students and amongst those adults generally who want to improve the quality of life. But this, unfortunately, is one of those instances where the word 'amateur' can spell great danger. Leaderless groups, or those with an untrained leader, risk doing very much more harm than good. Sometimes, through group members' well-meaning attempts to be 'frank' with each other, they can inflict deep wounds upon sensitive people, or strip them of defences without putting anything very useful in their place. At other times, they simply attract people who enjoy a chance to insult others, and who themselves need help which the amateur group is quite unfitted to give. Such groups never develop the positive regard and the empathic understanding towards their members which Rogers sees as being just as essential here as it is in the relationship between the individual therapist and his client. Even where amateur groups appear to be working successfully, they may sometimes only be encouraging forms of behaviour which, although they appear acceptable within the context of the group itself, are quite inappropriate in the everyday world outside, and will serve only to increase the disturbed person's sense of isolation from this world, and to make him morbidly overdependent upon the group instead of facing up to reality.

On balance, group therapy is something that has to be handled carefully, and is often best left in the guiding hands of the expert. The same is also true of *family therapy*, which is a form of group therapy involving only the members of the nuclear family. The focal point here is that the personality and general behaviour problems of a child (or often of an adult, for that matter) can only be correctly understood if the individual concerned is seen and treated within the context of his home circle – that is, within the context of his immediate psychological environment. Thus the child is seen by the therapist in the company of his parents, siblings, and any other members of his household. The family group is encouraged to speak freely about its tensions and difficulties, and about the way in which each person perceives and relates to the others, and gradually the causes of the child's problems (and of the problems he is in turn causing his family) are allowed to emerge. With greater understanding of each other's difficulties, the family becomes able to develop, with the help of the therapist, strategies of behaviour for putting things right (see Satir, 1972).

Achievement motivation

Once man has satisfied his basic biological needs, Lewin sees him as motivated most strongly by the need for social acceptance and status within his life space (this corresponds to the third need in Maslow's hierarchy). There are similarities here with Adler's concept of superiority (chapter 3). Most of what Maslow called man's meta needs, Lewin contends, stem from the way in which his psychological environment satisfies this need for social acceptance and for status. This is somewhat different from the humanistic psychologists' insistence that meta needs owe much of their strength to the individual's innate psychological endowment, but there would be little point in our pursuing this discussion, since there is no firm evidence either way. Both heredity and environment play a part in meta needs, but it is impossible to assign them their relative importance. It probably varies from need to need, and from person to person.

What is more relevant to the teacher is how psychologists actually investigate the need for social acceptance and status – or *achievement motivation*, as it is more generally called. Even more than Lewin himself, the psychologist who has been most active in this field is David McLelland (1961). Using a technique called content analysis, which counts the number of times particular themes recur, McLelland has analysed people's responses to projective tests, and has found that some people interpret such things as the TAT pictures (chapter 3) far more regularly in terms of achievement goals (for instance, 'He wants to succeed', 'She wants to be a doctor') than does the average person. These people are diagnosed by McLelland as being high on achievement motivation ('N'Ach' for short), and follow-up studies have shown that they do indeed set themselves higher than average goals, even taking ability and intelligence into account, and experience higher than average success in attaining them. More straightforward paper and pencil tests of N'Ach now exist, such as that of Mehrabian (1969).

A number of studies have shown the importance of social factors in prompting N'Ach in children. Generally, high N'Ach children have parents who encourage them to be independent, and to acquire new skills at a younger than average age; who avoid unnecessary restrictions in their upbringing; and who frequently use physical affection as a reward for achievement. For example, Rosen and d'Andrade (1959) found that parents of high N'Ach children not only gave their children more encouragement while watching them undertake a simple brick-building task than did parents of low N'Ach children, and gave them more affection on the task's successful completion, but also were far less likely to give them over-detailed instructions on how the job should be done, or to show irritation in the event of failure. (Certain obvious similarities suggest themselves between these parents and the parents of Coopersmith's high self-esteem boys described in chapter 2.)

McLelland has also produced interesting evidence to suggest the ways in which the school can encourage the low N'Ach child. He should be helped to set himself realistic and specific goals, to commit himself to them publicly, to talk about himself in the language of success rather than in that of failure, to recognise and acquire relevant skills, and to procure the support and encouragement of the classroom group.

Of course there is nothing new about any of these findings. They simply emphasise what we have been saying throughout about the child's need to be helped towards competence. There is, in fact, no real argument from the teacher's point of view between the field-theory approach to personality and the humanistic. As far as she is concerned at least, the one complements rather than contradicts the other.

Locus of control

Closely linked to humanistic and to field theories is the notion of *locus of control*. Locus of control (Rotter 1966) refers primarily to the way in which individuals view their successes and failures. Those with an external locus of control ascribe these things generally to external circumstances ('I did badly because my luck ran out', 'I failed because everyone was against me'), while those whose locus of control is internal feel the responsibility is generally their own ('I passed because I worked hard', 'It was my own fault I did so badly'). The origins of locus of control may be partly innate (temperamental), but certainly also owe much to social factors and learning. Not surprisingly, people whose locus of control is external seem often to prefer undertakings in which chance plays an important part, while people with an internal locus prefer opportunities to exercise personal qualities.

Clearly an exaggerated locus of control in either direction can be a bad thing. The tendency always to blame others can be a way of avoiding our own inadequacies, while always blaming ourselves can lead to feelings of personal worthlessness. The ideal is to view each situation with the objectivity and clarity that enables us to see why things are as they are, and then to get on with the business of making the best contribution we can.

Working along similar lines to Rotter, Weiner (most recently 1979) has developed what is known as *attribution theory*, which explores how we conceptualise and attribute the realms for success and failure in life. He shows that the most highly motivated students within formal education are those who prefer situations in which the consequences of their actions can be ascribed to themselves, attribute outcomes to personal effort, and are sensitive to cues that indicate the importance of effort expenditure in any area.

From the teacher's point of view, it would seem important, therefore, to help children understand that it is no good putting blame on others for one's own mistakes. Such a practice leads only to a distorted sense of reality and of one's own behaviour. The same is true of a tendency to ascribe everything to lucky or unlucky 'breaks'. Maturity of personality is only possible where individuals are helped to be honest with themselves and others, and to achieve the self-insight, and the realistic orientation towards the world, mentioned in chapter 3. At the same time, the teacher should be alert to an exaggerated internal locus of control, as manifested for example in the child who relies on his own efforts even when a request for help would be more appropriate, or the child who persists in judging himself harshly even when things are quite obviously not his fault.

6

The Trait-Based Approach

It is now time for us to turn our attention to what has become known as the trait-based approach to personality. This is sometimes referred to as the descriptive approach, because it is concerned to say what personality is like, rather than to speculate on its underlying psychological mechanisms as in the case of psychoanalytical and humanistic approaches.

In everyday language, when we describe people's personalities we use such words as 'friendly', 'confident', 'worried', and so on. These are known as *trait terms*, and Allport (1961) reports that no fewer than 4500 of them are in common use. This is a huge number, and on close inspection it is clear that most of them are really only describing different aspects of a much smaller number of underlying attributes. For example, a person's timidity, hesitancy, defensiveness and nervousness may all be due to a single attribute of anxiety. If we start hunting for these attributes, we are said to be adopting a *parsimonious* approach, an approach, much favoured in science, in which the observed facts are accounted for in terms of the smallest possible number of causes.

Such an approach is, in fact, no new thing in personality study. It stretches back at least as far as the Greek physician Galen in the second century AD, who saw all men as classifiable into four basic personality-types: the melancholic (sad and depressed), the phlegmatic (calm and stable), the choleric (irascible and quick-tempered), and the sanguine (cheerful and optimistic). It says something for the resilience of this theory that it was still going strong in the early twentieth century when the German

W. B. Wundt (1832–1920), one of the founding fathers of psychology, suggested that the four types could be explained by two basic bipolar traits: namely, strength of emotion (strong *versus* weak), and speed of emotional change (volatile *versus* stable). Thus, to Wundt, the melancholic person shows strong and stable emotions, the phlegmatic weak and stable, the choleric strong and volatile, and the sanguine weak and volatile. The importance of Wundt's theory is that it substitutes, for four rigid categories, two traits which can be expressed as scales or *dimensions*. Instead of being melancholic, *or* phlegmatic, *or* choleric, *or* sanguine, a person can now be placed at any point on the 'strong *versus* weak' and 'volatile *versus* stable' dimensions.

Whilst retaining the parsimony of Galen's approach, Wundt's model of personality is therefore much more able to explain individual differences. Instead of there being only four types of people, it gives us a wide variety spread out along the two dimensions, with only poeple at the extremes falling into Galen's four categories. The contemporary psychologist who has done most to develop Wundt's ideas is the British psychologist H. J. Eysenck, referred to several times already, and whom we must now study in more detail.

H. J. Eysenck

Eysenck readily acknowledges his debt to Wundt, but his work differs importantly in that it is based upon strong research evidence, which we shall be examining shortly. Eysenck, like Wundt, recognises the existence of two main personality traits or dimensions, but he considers them to be more correctly described by the terms *extroversion–introversion* (The 'E' dimension), and *neuroticism–stability* (the 'N' dimension). To these he has more recently added a third dimension, namely *high psychoticism – low psychoticism* (the 'P' dimension). Since an understanding of these various terms is essential for a grasp of Eysenck's personality theory, they require some discussion.

Extroversion–introversion Broadly, Eysenck accepts Jung's definition of the extrovert as a person who is oriented consciously towards the outer world of people and experiences. The typical extrovert is a person who makes friends readily, is fond of physical activity, likes change and variety in his life, is easily aroused emotionally but usually not very deeply, and tends to be materialistic, tough-minded and free from social inhibitions. Eysenck also accepts Jung's definition of the introvert as the direct opposite of these things, and far more inclined towards inner states of mind and intellectual pursuits.

What Eysenck does not accept (see, for instance, Eysenck and Eysenck 1969) is Jung's very complex view of personality, which he regards as impossibly elaborate and unscientific. He is particularly dismissive of Jung's theory (too lengthy to go into here) that the extrovert is always unconsciously introverted, and the introvert unconsciously extroverted. In fact, apart from his acceptance of Jung's definitions, Eysenck has very little in common with him.

Neuroticism–stability Neuroticism means, quite simply, a proneness to neurosis, to excessive anxiety, while stability indicates a relative freedom from it. Eysenck makes no attempt to subdivide anxiety into three different kinds as does Freud (chapter 3), and remains indeed very sceptical of most aspects of Freudian theory because he feels that they lie outside the scope of psychological proof. To Eysenck, who shares many sympathies with the behaviouristic thinking that we shall be examining in the next chapter, concepts such as the id and the super-ego remain little more than speculations.

Psychoticism Psychoticism refers to psychosis – that is, to mental illness (see chapter 10). However, high scores on the psychoticism dimension do not necessarily mean that the individual is psychotic, simply that he or she shows certain traits which are a feature of the psychotic but which are present in the normal population as well. The person with high scores on the psychoticism dimension tends to be somewhat unfeeling, insensitive, solitary, troublesome, and hostile, aggressive and even cruel towards others. He will generally be a sensation-seeker, enjoying arousal and danger, and may be something of a social misfit, with strong independence of behaviour and outlook (Eysenck and Eysenck 1976).

Measuring Eysenck's dimensions

Few people come out at the extreme ends of Eysenck's dimensions (for instance, as extremely extroverted or introverted). Most people cluster more towards the centre. Since the three dimensions are taken to explain all, or nearly all, of the observable differences in personality between people, it follows that everyone has a score of some kind on each dimension. Eysenck's results show that scores on the dimensions are not generally correlated, which means that a person's E score, for example, will tell us nothing about the score he is likely to get on the N dimension.

Because of this absence of correlation, the dimensions are said to be *orthogonal*, and in figure 2 the two most frequently explored dimensions (extroversion–introversion and neuroticism–stability) are represented diagrammatically by orthogonal reference axes. It will be seen from the diagram that people with scores at the extreme ends of the dimensions fall into four groups, characterised, as we proceed clockwise around the diagram, by extroversion, stability, introversion and neuroticism. By the same reckoning, people who have *both* their scores at the extreme ends

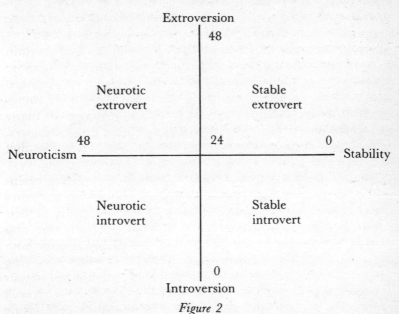

Figure 2

of dimensions will come out as stable extroverts, stable introverts, neurotic introverts, or neurotic extroverts. Eysenck suggests that these four categories correspond with Galen's sanguine, phlegmatic, melancholic and choleric people, respectively (which may make some people wonder just how far psychology *has* managed to advance in 2000 years!).

The majority of people, whose scores will fall short of the extreme ends of the dimensions, will still tend to fall within one of the four quarters of the diagram. You will need to score full marks for extroversion and full marks for neuroticism to become the epitome of the neurotic extrovert, but any score higher than 24 for extroversion and 24 for neuroticism will show that you have a tendency in this direction. The only 'neutral' person will be he whose scores lie at the precise mid-point of both dimensions (though you could, of course, score high or low on one dimension and yet remain neutral on the other).

The research evidence which has accumulated in support of Eysenck's dimensions comes not from devices with complicated and controversial methods of scoring, such as projective tests, but from simple questionnaires which ask people for details about their states of mind, and which can be objectively scored. In this sense, they share some similarities with the measurement techniques of the humanistic psychologists, but there the similarity between Eysenck and people such as Maslow and Rogers ends. As he does with the psychoanalysts, Eysenck tends to regard the humanistic psychologists as rather short on experimental evidence. The things they say about meta needs *may* be true, agrees Eysenck, or they may be fantasy. In the light of present knowledge, we have no real way of knowing.

Eysenck's own approach has been to present large samples of people with batteries of questions about themselves, and then to factor-analyse their responses. Results have convinced him that certain traits of personality tend to be found together (for instance, the person who is sociable tends also to be impulsive, carefree, talkative and lively), and it is three of these separate groups or clusters of attributes that he has identified as extroversion–introversion, neuroticism–stability, and psychoticism, respectively. Following on from the Maudsley Medical Questionnaire in 1952, Eysenck has produced the Maudsley Personality Inventory (1959), the Eysenck Personality Inventory (1964) and the Eysenck Personality Questionnaire (1975) together with variants of these tests for use with special groups (for example, the Junior Eysenck Personality Inventory, used with young children). A shortened version of the Maudsley Personality Inventory is given as table 2. The scoring key by the side of each question indicates whether a 'yes' answer would gain a score on the E dimension or on the N dimension.

Table 2   Short Form of the Maudsley Personality Inventory

		Key
A	Do you sometimes feel happy, sometimes depressed, without any apparent reason?	N
B	Do you have frequent ups and downs in mood, either with or without apparent cause?	N
C	Are you inclined to be moody?	N
D	Does your mind often wander while you are trying to concentrate?	N
E	Are you frequently 'lost in thought' even when supposed to be taking part in conversation?	N
F	Are you sometimes bubbling over with energy and sometimes very sluggish?	N
G	Do you prefer action to planning for action?	E
H	Are you happiest when you get involved in some project that calls for rapid action?	E
I	Do you usually take the initiative in making new friends?	E
J	Are you inclined to be quick and sure in your actions?	E
K	Would you rate yourself as a lively individual?	E
L	Would you be very unhappy if you were prevented from making many social contacts?	E

Reproduced with the permission of H. J. Eysenck.

The various versions of Eysenck's personality questionnaires have been extensively used in research in education and in other areas, such as management, crime, sexual behaviour and belief systems. In addition to items designed to measure the three dimensions already discussed, these questionnaires also contain a lie scale (the 'L' dimension) consisting of questions which truthful people tend to answer with the same response. Therefore anyone who gets more than a certain number of them 'wrong' can be assumed to be lying. Inevitably, we must then doubt the truthfulness of his responses to the other items in the Inventory. (Obviously, when attempting the test, the subject has no idea on which scale a particular question is marked, and may not even know that it contains a lie scale.) Recent research has shown that, although there is no correlation between L scores and either N or E scores, high L scorers do tend to be relatively lower in measured intelligence (IQ) and in self-insight. There is also evidence of a *negative* correlation between L scores and scores on the P (psychoticism) dimension (Eysenck and Eysenck 1976).

Personality dimensions and educational achievement

Since the 1960s, extensive studies have been carried out with children of all ages in an attempt to establish how scores on Eysenck's dimensions relate to educational achievement. For example, do extroverts perform better in school than introverts? Or stable children better than neurotic children? The potential utility of such studies is easy to recognise, but unfortunately results have been much less clear-cut than one would hope, and such trends as have been observed have been generally slight. The reason for this, as indicated by the work of Bennett and his colleagues (e.g. 1976, 1982), is that we have within the classroom a complex interaction between the child's own personality, the personality of the teacher, the teaching-methods employed, and the nature of the learning tasks that are being undertaken. It could be, to take hypothetical examples, that introverted children do better when taught by an introverted teacher using a formal teaching-style and teaching a subject such as English literature where individual work is the norm, but less well even with an introverted teacher if the subject is one which demands group work. On the other hand, extroverts might do better when the teacher herself is extroverted, and where the teaching-style is informal and the subject matter requires more in the way of corporate activity, but show little benefit from being taught by an extroverted teacher if the subject being taught demands introverted behaviour.

These examples serve to show how difficult it is to study the child's personality and educational performance in isolation from all the other things going on in the classroom (including, incidentally, the personalities of the other children). The best we can do in the light of current knowledge is to summarise some of the trends that appear to be discernible, and suggest their possible implications for the teacher, bearing in mind that much of what we say is tentative and that there will always be teachers and children who lie outside any generalisations we try to advance.

The first and most obvious point is that, if extroverts do enjoy social interaction and plentiful environmental stimuli, then they are likely to welcome a learning-context which allows for group work and for relatively frequent changes of occupation, while introverts may prefer a more individual and settled pattern of working. The lesson for the teacher here is that she must be sensitive to differences in personality amongst her children, and must try and provide a working environment sufficiently flexible to be able to accommodate these differences. It is all too easy for a teacher who is herself introverted to demand quiet individual working from her children, and to become impatient with those class members who find it hard to conform with this demand. Conversely it is equally easy for the extroverted teacher to lay great emphasis upon group work and classroom activity and to find herself out of sympathy with those children who find it hard to produce their best work under these circumstances.

The second point is that anxious children (children with high scores on the N dimension) may worry a great deal about their work and about such things as tests and examinations, to say nothing of teacher reprimands. A teacher who is herself a stranger to anxiety may regard such children as immature or foolish, and may have little sympathy for their very real distress. On the other hand, a teacher who is herself prone to anxiety may see stable and unanxious children as insensitive or as deliberately uncaring. Again the lesson here is for the teacher to study her children, to respect their individual differences, and not to censure them simply because their reactions to things diverge sharply from her own.

The third point is that although the E and the N dimensions are not correlated with each other, they nevertheless do inter-act with each other as we have already seen, producing as a consequence the four personality 'types' of stable extroverts, neurotic extroverts, stable introverts and neurotic introverts. From an educational point of view, each of these four types may react rather differently to the learning situation. Typically the neurotic extrovert is liable to uncontrolled behaviour, often making excessive demands upon others. Eysenck (1978) talks of him as being histrionic, with frequent mood changes, and with exaggerated emotional reactions (whether of anger, distress or whatever). As an extrovert, his orientation is primarily outwards, and this means that he will direct his neurotic problems outwards, seeking the company of others when troubled, either to ask their help or to take out his own troubled state of mind on them. The stable extrovert, whose orientation is also outwards, will by contrast direct affability and friendliness towards others, taking an interest in them for their own sake rather than as a way of enabling him to work through his personal problems.

In the classroom, therefore, the unstable extrovert may tend to be disruptive and quarrelsome in behaviour, or excessively emotionally overdependent, while the stable extrovert will tend to be cheerful and co-operative. Both will appear to need the company of others, but this need will be expressed in quite different ways. In terms of classroom control it will be the unstable extrovert, with his constant demands upon others, who will tend to cause the most problems, and he may also find it more difficult to develop the attention span and the kind of study habits that lead to successful educational attainment.

Similar contrasts exist with introversion. The neurotic introvert will tend towards brooding and self-examination, with an inclination to be lost in thought and to worry excessively over minor things. In the classroom he may be something of an isolate, quiet and shy and seeking solitude when upset. The stable introvert, however, though also oriented towards inner states of mind, will be tranquil and relaxed, capable of relating happily to others but very much at home in his own company, and in general showing a self-sufficiency that helps him develop a good attention span and good study habits.

Many children will not belong specifically to any one of these personality types since they will score at the mid-points of the dimensions concerned, but nevertheless significant numbers of them will show tendencies in one or other of the four directions, and in the classroom it is not difficult for the teacher to recognise these tendencies. Once they have been recognised, the task of the teacher is not so much to try and change them as to help children recognise these tendencies in themselves, and to provide children, as already indicated, with learning-environments which take full account of their individual differences. As we shall see shortly, when we discuss the physiology of Eysenck's dimensions, it may be that innate factors play an important part in how extroverted or neurotic we are, and that scope for change is in any case limited. But, limited or not, it would be wrong to try and force children into a particular personality mould simply because this is the one that most closely accords with the teacher's own or because this is the one that she finds most conducive to her way of running things.

Also of relevance to the teacher is the fact that extroversion is subject to an age effect, tending to peak at around age ten and eleven and then to show a steady decline through adolescence. Thus the bubbling and exuberant child at the top end of the junior school often in the course of two or three years turns into the rather withdrawn and pensive teenager. From an educational point of view this has some advantage, in that as children grow older we expect more individual work from them in any case, and their increasing tendency towards introversion makes them better able to cope with such demands. By the time the stage of higher education is reached, there is a very definite premium upon long periods of sustained work on one's own, and evidence suggests that the introvert may in consequence have important benefits in terms of study habits. Particularly at risk it would appear is the unstable extrovert, since he tends to seek company as a way of forgetting his worries, and as a result may find it very difficult indeed to get down to work during the anxious period before examinations.

Interestingly, although the advantage gained by introverts holds for both artists and scientists at the higher-education level and in adult life generally, it is particularly marked for scientists, perhaps because even more of their work is solitary than is the case with the artist. Successful scientists seem generally to have lower N scores than successful artists, however, suggesting perhaps that on occasions high N scores may go with the kind of sensitivity necessary for artistic criticism and expression (see Eysenck 1983 for a review of relevant findings).

Anxiety and educational achievement   In spite of this possible link between above average N scores and success in certain arts subjects, the teacher must nevertheless be careful not to arouse anxiety in children unnecessarily. We know that, high N scores and artistic success apart, a *mild* degree of anxiety can improve motivation and performance, but that once anxiety increases beyond this optimum level it may have an inhibiting effect. It appears also that, the more complex the task, the more likely it is that this inhibiting effect will occur. Thus anxiety-provoking situations such as tests and examinations may well prevent many children from performing at their best, particularly where these tests and examinations demand the recall of detailed abstract material (as, for example, in science subjects and foreign languages). What raises anxiety to this inhibiting level in one child may simply act as a useful motivator to another, however, which often means that particularly stressful events such as public examinations are regrettably as much a way of testing children's nerves as they are of testing their knowledge.

There is little that the teacher can do about the fact of public examinations, but she can help to lessen the anxiety they cause by seeing to it that pupils are well prepared for them, have had ample practice in examination technique, and are encouraged to discuss and come to terms with their anxieties. Such anxieties should never be dismissed as groundless or as signs of weakness. They are real enough to the child who is experiencing them, and his prime need is for a sympathetic and understanding teacher who will assist him in looking objectively at his worries and in trying to keep them in proportion.

School-based tests and examinations are a different matter, however, and here the teacher and the school generally should think carefully about the purpose that lies behind them. Tests and examinations can be either of the *summative* kind or of the *formative* kind. Summative tests are attainment tests designed to find out how much the child knows and to compare him against a particular standard, while formative tests are aimed more at giving the teacher feedback on what has been learnt and on helping her establish how learning can be made more effective (Fontana 1984). In a summative test, a child knows that he is in a sense on trial, and will be subject to anxiety accordingly, whereas in a formative test he knows there is no pressure of this kind and that the whole exercise is simply designed to further his own progress. As pointed out by Bloom (1983) and other authorities, schools tend to use tests primarily for summative rather than for formative purposes, seeing them as a way of motivating children to learn rather than as a way of finding out how learning can best be helped to take place. The result is that such tests do very little to benefit the majority of children, serving often to fill them with a sense of failure and/or to make them feel nervous and anxious about the subject matter and their relationships with the teachers concerned.

Research evidence to date With the above guidelines and reservations firmly in mind, we can now summarise available research evidence on specific links between Eysenck's dimensions and educational success. The findings of a range of large-scale studies both in Britain and in the USA (see Kline 1983 for a summary) show that in the primary school stable extroverted children do best. The correlations between this personality type and academic success are consistently significant at this age level, though their smallness reminds us again that there are many other factors involved in addition to those of personality. At the secondary-school stage, the picture gradually changes (perhaps more rapidly for girls than for boys), with introversion becoming increasingly important, particularly in the sciences. This is probably owing to the growing emphasis in the secondary school upon individual work, to which I have already drawn attention. But it may be that the age-related trend towards introversion mentioned earlier also plays a part, in that, as Anthony (1973) suggests, successful extroverts in the primary school may have developed into successful introverts by the time they are immersed in secondary schooling.

As we suggested earlier in the chapter, by the time higher education is reached, though even here the correlations with academic success are still neither large nor clear-cut, there appears to be a further premium upon introversion. Studies from the USA suggest that it is the stable introvert who is most favoured, though in Britain the question of whether it is the stable or the unstable introvert who does best remains more open to debate. Some evidence, as we have seen, suggests that stability may be a help in science and engineering (perhaps because these subjects handle precise complex data where high anxiety levels could be a handicap to performance) but less so in arts subjects (where sometimes greater emphasis is placed upon sensitivity towards the expression and communication of emotions). Be this as it may, it would seem as if in both science and arts subjects unstable extroversion tends to go least readily with academic success (Wankowski 1970). We have already identified a possible explanation for this in observing that the unstable extrovert is prone to seek company as a way of forgetting his worries. His extrovert need for social stimuli when faced with the high anxiety of preparing for examinations may make it very difficult for him to get down to the lonely, sustained work which such preparation demands. As a consequence he may more readily be found down in the student bar or pestering his friends when the tensions mount, and it is therefore this personality type who may need particularly careful support from his teachers at stressful times.

The physiology of Eysenck's dimensions

It was observed at the beginning of this chapter that Eysenck shows little interest in formulating theories on the underlying mechanisms of personality in the manner of the psychoanalysts and the humanistic psychologists. However, with his belief that at least 70 per cent of the personality differences between people revealed by the Maudsley and the Eysenck Personality Inventories are owing to heredity, he has shown a keen concern to isolate the physiological factors involved (see, for instance, Eysenck 1983; Fontana 1983). This research is only of interest to teachers in those areas where it throws direct light upon children's behaviour, and we therefore have no need to go into it in any great depth. Briefly, he suggests that anxiety is particularly associated with the autonomic nervous system (i.e. that system that operates without any conscious volition on the part of the individual, and controls such things as digestion, sweating, blood pressure and heart rate), and with the hypothalamus area of the brain, which helps to arouse it. Some people, quite simply, may have a more sensitive and easily aroused autonomic nervous system than others. There is some evidence, for example, that ectomorphs (see chapter 1) and women may be more highly endowed in this sphere.

Of interest to the teacher is the suggestion put forward by Lynn (1971) that those children who have a naturally *sluggish* autonomic nervous system (and who would therefore have a low N score) may get a definite thrill from the arousal associated with anxiety (Freud would say this is the thanatos at work!), and may seek this arousal by taking risks that the nervous child would steer well clear of. These risks could be obvious physical ones such as climbing trees and rough play, or they could be more subtle ones such as baiting the teacher or teasing other children. Since, if this is the case, it would seem wrong for the school to clamp down on risk-taking altogether, it should be channelled into acceptable areas such as organised games and outdoor adventure pursuits.

As to extroversion–introversion, Eysenck suggests that the reticular formation area of the brain may be the main physiological cause. This is the part of the brain that helps to stimulate and inhibit the cortex and thus to control the individual's state of attention and wakefulness. In Eysenck's submission, the reticular formation of the introvert allows him to build up inhibition more slowly than does that of the extrovert. He therefore can concentrate for longer periods on the same repetitive task. He can also remain more sensitive to the constant, subtle signals of his own thoughts and feelings. Note that the word 'inhibition' in this context has nothing to do with social inhibition. It simply means that the introvert remains much less resistant to the stream of sensory messages that come at him from the environment and from within himself. He therefore needs far fewer of them. He remains satisfied with a good book, or with his own thoughts, or with his record-player played softly, whereas the extrovert quickly gets immune to these things and looks for new sources of stimulation.

Eysenck also notes that the introvert, again perhaps because his lower inhibition level renders him more sensitive to the stimuli concerned, picks up conditioned responses (chapter 8) more rapidly than does the extrovert. This means he learns more quickly – not only, perhaps, those things to do with academic work, but also social rules and regulations. This may be why there is a significant correlation between extroversion (particularly unstable extroversion) and crime. The extrovert may just not be as aware of social codes as is the introvert. Or, more particularly, he may not be as aware of the *need* for these things as is the introvert. What could also contribute here is the fact that, because he is less sensitive towards his own feelings, he may be less able to empathise with others, and therefore to be sensitive towards their needs and their rights.

These physiological factors may also explain why extroverts are generally higher on aggression and on leadership qualities than are introverts, and also why at all ages men are more inclined towards extroversion than are women. (Interestingly, extroverts are also more inclined to be mesomorphic than are introverts – another reason, as we saw in chapter 1, for thinking that heredity may play some part in the matter.) But all this evidence in favour of inheritance must not make us lose sight of the fact that Eysenck sees a very substantial percentage of people's scores on his dimensions to be owing to environment. As he rejects the psychoanalytical or the humanistic explanation for the interaction between heredity and environment, he adopts instead the learning-theory model, which we shall be looking at in the next chapter.

The psychoticism dimension

As yet the psychoticism dimension has not been used so extensively for research within education as have the other two dimensions isolated by Eysenck, and the evidence upon which we have to go has therefore been derived primarily from work with adults. The most significant aspect of this evidence is probably that a link appears to exist between high P scores and creativity for both undergraduate students and for practising artists (Eysenck 1983). This may be because the personality characteristics that appear to go with high P scores (independence, solitariness, tough-mindedness, aggression and the like) are helpful aids towards artistic success, at least in Western societies. But, as with most research involving large samples of people and the use of personality questionnaires, we must point out that a link of this kind does not mean that people with low P scores are excluded from becoming creative artists. The link is a statistical one, and simply indicates that amongst creative people there are rather more high P scorers than one would expect to find purely on the grounds of chance.

Nevertheless, this helps alert the teacher to the fact that sometimes creative children may not be the easiest of classmates, a point to which we shall be returning when we discuss creativity more fully in chapter 7. Creativity by definition involves an independent and original approach to life, and sometimes the creative person has to show a touch of ruthlessness in giving his creative work precedence over the social demands made upon him by others. If we want creativity in children, we have to remember that on occasions it may have its less comfortable side.

R. B. Cattell

Another important advocate of the trait-based approach is R. B. Cattell. Cattell argues that his own research, conducted along similar lines to that of Eysenck, and again using factor analysis, reveals the existence of many more than two or three dimensions. On the basis of his findings, he has constructed a number of personality inventories, namely the Sixteen Personality Factor Questionnaire (16PF), which measures the sixteen traits or dimensions that he claims exist in adults; the High School Personality Questionnaire, which measures the fourteen that are identifiable in children from twelve to eighteen; the Child's Personality Quiz, which is for ages eight to twelve; the Early School Personality Quiz, for children of six to eight years of age; and the Pre-School Personality Quiz for children of four to six years (Cattell and Kline 1977).

The terms that Cattell uses for his dimensions (or factors, as he calls them) are a little daunting, but the fourteen that figure in his High School Personality Questionnaire are given, with translations, in table 3. It will be noted that Cattell uses some psychoanalytical language, but he has little else in common with the psychoanalytical approach. His differences with Eysenck, on the other hand, are more apparent than real, since he accepts that many of his factors do correlate with each other, and that they can be grouped into a few broad categories, or *source traits*, which look very much like Eysenck's dimensions, and of which the two most important are extroversion and anxiety.

Cattell's tests have been used more widely in the USA but less widely in Britain than those of Eysenck, and it remains to

Table 3   Factors in Cattell's High School Personality Questionnaire

A	Affectothymia (sociable)	–	Schizothymia (reserved)
B	High intelligence	–	Low intelligence
C	Ego strength (stability)	–	Low ego strength (instability)
D	Excitability	–	Phlegmatism
E	Dominance (self-assertion)	–	Submissiveness
F	Surgency (exuberance)	–	Desurgency (sobriety)
G	Strong super-ego (conscientiousness)	–	Weak super-ego
H	Parmia (venturesomeness)	–	Threctia (shyness)
I	Premsia (sensitivity)	–	Harria (toughness)
J	Coasthenia (individuality)	–	Zeppia (group involvement)
O	Guilt proneness	–	Confidence
Q2	Self-sufficiency	–	Group dependency
Q3	Controlled	–	Uncontrolled
Q4	High ergic tension (tense)	–	Low ergic tension (relaxed)

be seen which, in the long run, will prove the more useful. To date, Cattell's have certainly produced a much more confusing picture when employed within education than have Eysenck's, and there would be little point in reviewing the evidence since it does not add much to what has already been said in this chapter. Suffice it to say that when Rushton (1966) employed the Cattell measures in British primary schools, he found only factors C, F and G correlated with educational achievement, but that, when the results were reanalysed in terms of the source traits of extroversion and anxiety, much the same relationship with achievement was revealed as with Eysenck's E and N.

Other personality-measuring devices

Numerous other personality questionnaires exist besides those of Eysenck and Cattell, some designed to measure the total personality, and others designed to measure specific aspects of it. One of the best known examples of the former, from which a number of the latter have been derived, is the Minnesota Multiphasic Personality Inventory (or MMPI), devised by Hathaway and McKinley in 1943. It consists of no fewer than

550 statements, such as 'I brood a great deal', 'I'm entirely self-confident', to which the subject responds with a simple 'True'/'False'. The test is an interesting one, because in a way it bridges the gap between the idiographic and the nomothetic approaches to personality. It has been derived not from factor analysis, but from a comparison between the typical responses of mentally ill and normal people respectively to the items it contains. It yields nine scales indicative of different kinds of mental disorder (e.g. depression, paranoia, hysteria), and the results provide a 'profile' of the individual's mental health.

The MMPI is used more widely in clinical than in educational psychology, but many of the tests that have been based wholly or in part upon questions taken from it have considerable application to education. Space only allows three examples.

The California Psychological Inventory, introduced by Gough in 1957, is regarded by many as one of the best personality tests in existence. Sometimes known as the sane man's MMPI, it contains 480 items designed to measure normal personality, and yields fifteen scales which can be grouped under the three headings of 'poise and self-assurance', 'sociability and maturity', and 'achievement and aptitude'.

The Manifest Anxiety Scale (MAS), devised by Taylor in 1953, contains fifty items (plus 175 'buffer' items that are not scored) designed to measure anxiety. It has proved particularly useful in examining the relationship between anxiety and learning performance. As we should predict from our earlier discussion, subjects with high MAS scores do better on simple learning-tasks than do those with low scores, but less well on complex tasks.

The California F Scale, devised principally by Adorno in 1950, is designed to measure the authoritarian personality, which, on the basis of responses to the MMPI and to projective tests such as the TAT (see chapter 3), Adorno suggests is characterised by conformity, submissiveness (to superiors), dominance (to inferiors), aggression, superstition, destructiveness, cynicism, and an exaggerated and repressive concern with sex. Originally containing thirty-nine items, the F Scale has undergone some rather *ad hoc* revisions. It invites a simple 'True'/'False' response to such statements as 'Obedience and the respect for authority are the most important virtues children can learn', and '. . . criminals ought to be publicly whipped or worse'.

The F Scale has generated a great deal of research, and of particular interest to the teacher are findings that in his dealings with children the authoritarian personality is rigid, stereotyped and unsympathetic. Because he is unable to tolerate ambiguity (like the conformist people in Asch's experiments mentioned in chapter 4), he is unable to allow children to experiment enough to find the essential balance between individuality and conventionality. Freud would argue, of course, that this authoritarian behaviour is a defence mechanism indicative of a rigidly over-controlled ego, and that the authoritarian personality is really suffering from neurotic and moral anxiety. His exaggeratedly 'correct' attitude is probably also a sign of the defence mechanism of reaction formation.

Support for this view would seem to come from the fact that authoritarian parents (and teachers?) tend to produce authoritarian children (Kelvin 1970). By their inflexible attitude towards their children, authoritarian people may well awaken in them precisely the kind of over-controlling super-ego that has led to their own problems.

Attitude-testing

Tests such as the F Scale bring us to an area which has certain similarities to the trait-based approach – namely, attitude-testing. It will be remembered that in the definition of personality adopted in the Introduction, attitudes were mentioned as one of the things that render each man's personality unique. We may share many of our attitudes with other people – our family, our colleagues, our political party – but the exact permutation of attitudes that we hold is distinctive to ourselves.

Attitudes can be defined as the reasonably enduring orientations which people develop towards the objects and issues they encounter in life, and which they express verbally in their *opinions*. Obviously attitudes contain elements of value and of belief, and psychoanalysts would argue that we hold both conscious and unconscious ones. Often when we are employing ego-defence mechanisms such as reaction formation, conscious and unconscious attitudes may be at complete variance with each other. Unconsciously, for example, a child may have a hostile attitude towards a younger sibling, but this so outrages the idea of brotherly love which his parents have incorporated into his super-ego that consciously he adopts a particularly protective and solicitous attitude towards him.

Attitudes are normally measured in one of two ways. Either through a 'True'/'False' response to a number of statements of opinion such as those of the F Scale (a variant of the 'True'/ 'False' response is a five-point scale from 'Strongly agree' down to 'Strongly disagree'), or through non-directional scales such as the Osgood Semantic Differential (see chapter 4), where the individual chooses which adjectives in his opinion best describe the issue under scrutiny. Obviously, these tests measure conscious rather than unconscious attitudes, though psychoanalysts claim that the latter can often be revealed if the individual freely associates to his consciously chosen adjectives.

Not surprisingly in view of his general approach to personality, Eysenck considers there may be a few dimensions which underlie all our conscious attitudes. In his Social Attitude Inventory, devised in 1954, he claims to be measuring a conservative–radical dimension, and a tough–tender-minded one. Fascists, it is argued, tend to be tough-minded and conservative, communists tough-minded and radical, and liberals tender-minded and radical.

Through identification (see chapter 2), children assimilate most of their attitudes initially from their parents, and later from teachers and peer groups. They probably also get them from books, television and the media generally. Teachers are often very concerned about this, and wonder at the extent to which children can develop undesirable attitudes through the media's predilection for violence and general lawless activity. Surprisingly, in spite of numerous pieces of well-publicised research, we are still not sure. Bandura (whom we shall be looking at in chapter 8) shows that children certainly sometimes act out the kinds of violence that they have just been watching, but whether a non-violent child could be made into a violent one simply by what he sees on the television is quite another matter.

As children discover identity in adolescence, so their attitudes tend to become more stable, and this process goes on throughout life, so that many people in late adult life prove very resistant to attempts to change their way of thinking. However, in all of us attitudes sometimes change quite sharply if for some reason or other we find ourselves having to resist things that threaten what Kelly (see chapter 7) would call our *core constructs*. This is particularly apparent in research connected with the theory of cognitive dissonance.

Cognitive-dissonance theory is associated particularly with the work of Leon Festinger. It has to do with the conscious holding by the individual of two attitudes (or ideas or bits of information) which conflict (are in dissonance with) each other, as when, for example, a person has confidence in his abilities in a certain subject, yet finds himself failing an examination which he believes is a just measure of these abilities. Since such dissonance is difficult to live with, the individual usually reduces it by modifying one of the dissonant attitudes (e.g. he might say the exam is no good after all). Festinger calls this a *dissonance-reducing change*. To bring about such a change, people are sometimes prepared greatly to distort their true pictures of the outside world (e.g. there may be overwhelming evidence that the exam *is* a valid measure). A person who is insecure or low in self-esteem may go to great lengths to distort reality in order to preserve his precarious self-concepts and other core constructs. Rogers (see chapter 4) would say that he allows incongruence to develop between his phenomenal field and the outside world.

Once having made a dissonance-reducing change, we all seek to lower dissonance still further by interpreting all new evidence in terms of this change (e.g. the discovery that the exam syllabus is being changed next year would be taken as 'proof' that this year's exam was unsatisfactory). Festinger claims that dissonance-reducing changes are particularly prone to happen when people have taken irrevocable decisions. Thus, in an experiment by one of his associates, Jecker, it was demonstrated that a sample of girls each improved their individual ratings of pop records (which in fact they liked only moderately) immediately after they have been manoeuvred into choosing them as free gifts (Festinger 1962). The girls, it seemed, could not support the dissonance of not liking the records much and yet having chosen them as gifts, so they reduced it by convincing themselves the records were good ones after all.

Dissonance-reducing changes are also prone to happen after one has told a lie. To reduce the gap between public statement and private information, the tendency is to tamper with the latter to bring it in line with the former. Thus one is able to tell oneself that it wasn't *really* a lie at all. This tendency, it seems, is particularly marked if the lie has brought little significant reward. It is as if our core constructs of ourselves as basically truthful people can survive more easily if we see ourselves as giving way to strong temptation (as in telling a lie that brings a big reward) rather than as giving way to weak.

Festinger sees the desire to reduce dissonance as a significant motivating-factor in human behaviour. Since dissonance is unpleasant, it sets up tensions in us that we very much want to reduce. It may be that future research will show us that the authoritarian personality, who as we have seen has a low toleration of ambiguity, takes up his dogmatic stance partly because it removes the necessity for choice, and therefore removes the dissonance which is sometimes consequent upon choice. It could be that we shall also find that people who avoid ever making important decisions do so partly because, through their insecurity, they have a low tolerance of dissonance (such findings would fit in well with psychoanalytical theory). We might also find, in the reverse direction, that people who can tolerate an abnormally high level of dissonance are just as insecure, preferring to be chronically two-faced rather than to tackle the disagreements with other people that consistent attitudes sometimes bring (or they could lack any moral sense, like the psychopath we shall be looking at in chapter 10).

Personality measurement and educational guidance

Most of the measuring-devices that we have been looking at in this chapter have been standardised with large samples of people. This means that norms and standard deviations have been obtained for them which allow us to say how far the test results of any one individual differ from those of the average person. If this standardisation were not done, we would find ourselves asking what a particular score on, say, the F Scale actually means.

Does it mean that the person is more or less authoritarian than the average, and if so by how much?

Standardised tests of this kind are of particular use when it comes to educational and vocational guidance. Some of the most widely used of such tests are the British Social Adjustment Guides (Stott 1963), in which the teacher underlines the descriptions of behaviour that apply to a child she suspects is suffering from personality problems. These ratings are then analysed to see how far they depart from norms which have been obtained for children generally, and a diagnosis of the extent of the child's problems is made.

Also useful in educational guidance are tests which measure children's interests, such as the Edwards Personal Preference Schedule (Edwards 1953). Based on fifteen of the 'needs' suggested by Murray (see chapter 3), such as achievement, aggression and autonomy, it contains 210 pairs of statements between which the child has to choose: for instance, 'I like to be successful in things', 'I like to make new friends.' His results are then presented in terms of the relative strength of these needs.

Such tests can be used in vocational guidance, but they are less good than those designed specifically for the purpose. Rosenberg's Occupations and Values Test (1957) divides subjects into those oriented towards people, towards extrinsic rewards (money, status), and towards intrinsic rewards (creativity, self-expression). The Rothwell–Miller Interest Blank (1968) divides them into twelve job categories, such as outdoor, scientific, social-service, mechanical, clerical and medical, and then lists a wide variety of jobs in each of these categories. These jobs cover various levels of intelligence and attainment. Thus, for example, a person whose interests place him in the 'mechanical' category would have a choice of jobs ranging from civil engineer to petrol-pump attendant. Increasingly, the kind of material contained in these tests is being built into computer programmes, thus producing more flexibility and subject participation (see Watts 1978).

Of general use in educational guidance and assessment are tests of academic motivation, of which two of the best are those of Entwistle. His Aberdeen Academic Motivation Inventory (1968) is designed for use in secondary schools, while his Student's Attitudes Inventory (1971) is for higher education.

These tests are really measures of attitudes towards academic work, and the latter also yields scores on study habits, examination technique, and lack of distraction. Like all attitude tests they measure only conscious attitudes, of course, and are susceptible to faking, but within these limits seem sound diagnostic devices.

At the primary-school level, a comparable though broader test which yields scores on such things as attitudes to school, interest in school work, attitudes to class, social adjustment, relationship with teacher, and self-image, is that of Barker Lunn (1969).

Criticisms of the trait approach

From the educational point of view, one of the questions that has to be asked of any psychological approach is how useful is it in helping the teacher work with children. One weakness of certain aspects of the trait-based approach is that, although it enables us to look for broad tendencies (e.g. those who show up as extroverts on Eysenck's personality questionnaires *tend* to do better in primary school than do introverts) it does not give us much information on individual children (e.g. many introverts do perfectly well in the primary school). The tendencies identified are often so slight that, although statistically significant when dealing with large samples, they are of very limited value when trying to predict how given individuals will fare. In addition, the trait-based approach often fails to tease out the complex range of variables that will influence what happens in particular instances. For example, we may find a whole class of children going against the trend identified by trait research simply because they have a rather unorthodox teacher who produces unorthodox results. Or we may find that a sudden change in the content of a syllabus will produce radical changes in children's response and in their success rate, or that the coming of a new and popular teacher or of modifications to the examination system will change things.

Another criticism of the trait approach is that it tells us nothing about the unconscious or about meta needs and long-term goals and aspirations. Trait theorists will argue that this is because such things are too vague for precise measurement, but this ignores the fact that in the individual's own life they may be of paramount importance. Then again it is sometimes argued that trait methods are an oversimplification. As we have seen, Freud for example divided anxiety into three different kinds, and it could therefore be that a single anxiety score such as that yielded by Eysenck's questionnaires is of limited value and at times even misleading.

Similarly it is argued that research into attitudes gives us only a simplified and superficial picture of the individual as he really is. There is surprisingly little evidence that attitudes as measured by attitude questionnaires are actually reflected in behaviour. Thus a person who expresses highly moral attitudes in response to a questionnaire (or even in life generally) may be highly immoral in his actual behaviour. He knows the social desirability of expressing moral views in public, but is quite unable in his private life to live up to these ideals. Similarly people may have negative attitudes towards smoking or overeating or laziness or alcohol or smacking their children, yet be quite incapable of giving up the practices themselves. It is also said that the very act of 'measuring' an attitude gives it an appearance of permanence which in fact it does not possess.

Lastly, it is sometimes argued that human personality is not consistent enough to be assessed in terms of enduring traits. People fluctuate as they move from one environment to another and as the weeks and months go by. We saw an indication of this more flexible approach to personality when we discussed field and social models in chapter 5. But as we take up the issue in depth in the next chapter nothing further need be said about it here.

Each of these criticisms of the trait approach has some force behind it. But they tell us not that the trait approach should be discounted, but that in a complex area such as personality no single approach must be allowed to stand on its own. We can learn something of value from them all, and in the end it must be left to the individual to decide whether the trait approach or one of the other approaches that we look at in this book is the most appropriate in any given instance.

7

The State-Based Approach

In this chapter we look at an approach to personality that differs quite sharply from the trait-based approach discussed in chapter 6. The reader may indeed find it hard to reconcile the two, and be forced to make a decision as to which of them is of most practical help in the classroom. This apparent incompatibility stems from the fact that the state-based approach largely rejects the notion of fixed personality traits (compare the social models in chapter 5), and sees personality (and the mental and emotional experiences which underlie it) as in a continual state of flux and development. This accords well with the humanistic approach discussed in chapter 4, since humanistic psychologists also see personality as a changing, developing thing, but even here there is something of a variation in approach in that the state-based psychologists do not attempt to construct somewhat speculative models of personality, involving concepts such as meta needs, in the manner of the humanists. Instead, they are content to explore man *as he is* from moment to moment, using for the purpose measuring-devices which are claimed to be every bit as precise as those used by trait theorists.

This wide use of measuring-devices might lead us to suppose, in fact, that state theorists are simply trait theorists under a different name. Measuring-devices are only applicable, it might be said, if we are looking at fixed characteristics such as traits. But this is not so, and an analogy might help here, though like all analogies it must not be pushed too far. The measuring-devices used by trait theorists are analogous to rulers, enduring units of measurement designed to measure enduring qualities. Those of the state theorists, on the other hand, are analogous to thermometers, designed to measure qualities that fluctuate even from hour to hour. Of course, since rulers and thermometers are equally useful in their separate ways, this suggests a possible strategy for reconciling trait- and state-based approaches. It may be that the personality does have enduring traits, as argued by Eysenck and Cattell, but that it also has fluctuating qualities as argued by the state theorists.

While not denying that this may be a useful way of looking at personality from the pragmatic viewpoint of the teacher, with sometimes the trait-based model appearing more helpful and sometimes the state-based, it is right to point out that many state-based theorists would reject this compromise on the grounds that the notion of fixed states in any area of human psychology is a fundamental flaw in our way of looking at man, and is a particular handicap when it comes to working with and assessing the potential of children. As Thomas and Harri-Augstein (1985) put it, this handicap prompts us to mistake 'ineffective stabilised states in individuals and groups for permanent features', and by our mistake to perpetuate them. Learning-failures, low intelligence, personality traits and problems are therefore in the view of many state theorists the creation of the psychologists who purport to 'measure' these states, and in doing so beguile us into thinking we are looking at something fixed and solid like mountains when in fact we are looking at something shifting and changing like clouds. By the reckoning of the state theorists, human potential is a largely undiscovered quantity, and it is only by attempting to 'assess' it and to give it a fixed score that we (as with, for example, a low intelligence score) limit it. The limitation comes from the way in which we then react to the person who has been 'assessed'. We label him as of low intelligence or as of an unstable personality, and then by treating him accordingly and getting him to believe in the label and apply it to himself we serve to perpetuate it and cripple his chances of change and progress.

To some teachers this might seem rather an extreme view. Certainly many educational procedures are based upon the conviction that there are in children relatively enduring factors of personality and ability, and, indeed, if there were not it would make it impossible to 'know' someone in any realistic sense.

However, the state theorist would counsel us to realise that we must not confuse 'enduring' with 'fixed'. A quality may have been enduring up to now, but this does not mean that it cannot change or be helped to change, even in the short-term. And its very endurance may be less a feature of the quality itself than of the way in which, after the labelling-process has taken place, we and the person concerned persist in viewing him. Thus, with, for example, a quality such as anxiety, it may be that, although one individual may be innately more prone to experience this emotion than another, the fact that he has been labelled 'anxious' prevents him from believing in and learning the strategies that would help him develop beyond his anxiety reactions. In any case, state theorists would argue that it is far more useful to find out what situations arouse his anxiety, and how he himself perceives this anxiety, than simply to saddle him with a score on an anxiety inventory and then assume this tells us something permanent about his personality.

It will be apparent from what we have said that the state theorist views personality as a *process* rather than as a static element. We recognise that John is John and Mary is Mary simply because the processes of change are, in certain areas, sufficiently slow to allow us to see similarities in them as people from day to day – rather in the way in which we identify summer as summer, even though we know that there are changes in the weather several times daily, and that overall there is a gradual change from springtime into autumn. This means, of course, that state theorists, in addition to placing more emphasis upon the possibility of change and development in the personality, also take more account of fluctuating qualities such as moods and emotions, all of which are of great practical interest to the teacher.

The work of George Kelly

George Kelly (1905–1966) is one of the key figures – some would say, *the* key figure – in the state-based approach. Over the last two decades, his work has had a major impact upon educational psychology, and upon other important areas of applied psychology such as clinical and industrial psychology. Kelly's starting-up point (see, for instance, Bannister and Fransella 1980) is the premise that behind all man's other needs is the urge to explore the world. He explores it for food and drink, and when these needs are satisfied he goes on exploring it – for social relationships, for positive regard, for self-esteem, and in the end for the sake of exploration itself. Man is eternally curious. He wants to find out about the world, and he wants to make sense of what he finds. So far, this may not seem much of an advance over humanistic psychologists such as Maslow and Rogers, but where Kelly makes a major contribution to our thinking about personality is in his claim that we make sense of our phenomenal field, of our own subjective world, by forming what he calls *personal constructs* about it.

A personal construct is a unit of meaning, a unit which contains all the perceptions, interpretations and evaluations which the individual attaches to a particular event, or place, or person, or set of persons. For example, a child will have a construct labelled 'home', which consists of ideas and memories of what his home looks like, of the people who live there, of the activities that go on there, of the attitudes it arouses in him. Similarly, he holds constructs of 'school', of 'friends', of 'maths', of 'stamp-collecting' and so on. Because of its perceptual content, and because of the personal memories that it contains, a construct is rather more all-embracing than a concept. By means of our constructs, we understand the present and we are able to *anticipate* or *predict* the future. Without constructs, we should literally have to start afresh each day, and learn about the world all over again. But, because each person inhabits his own subjective world, we each build up constructs that are unique to ourselves. No two people ever share an identical construct.

We can see how this works if we go back to the point about two sincere witnesses giving conflicting accounts of the same event. Suppose the event is a playground fight, and a teacher is listening to varying accounts of who started it and who got hurt most. Kelly would say the varying accounts are caused by the fact that the witnesses hold differing constructs of the key elements involved, such as the participants, the desirability of fighting, the sanctity of the school rule which the participants may be breaking, the head teacher who will any moment arrive to deal out retribution, and so on. The older we become, the better we are able to sort out which constructs are relevant to any particular happening, but we still see the world through our own eyes, and not through anyone else's.

Construct theory can also help explain the effectiveness with which a child learns and remembers. When he tackles work, for example in geography, he brings to the task not only innate ability but also his construct 'geography', which will include all the geography teachers he has known, his attitude to other countries and races, the time it usually takes him to do his geography homework, the people he sits near in geography, the pleasantness of the geography room and much more besides. If this construct is on the whole a favourable one, then his motivation to explore geography will be high.

Many of the items that go to make up 'geography' will also be a part of other constructs as well. The child will have constructs of 'teachers', of 'books', of 'homework', of 'people I sit near' and so on, and the favourability or otherwise of these constructs will all inevitably influence 'geography'. However, as the construct 'geography' becomes stronger, so it will place more and more of a stamp on its own constituent elements. 'Geography teacher' will become dislodged from the construct 'teachers', and will come to belong more and more to the construct 'geography'. Thus, when the child comes to hear the term 'geography teacher' mentioned, he may react to it more positively than he will, say, to the term 'history teacher'.

Kelly (1955) lists a number of categories into which constructs can fall. Some of the most important of these are

impermeable constructs, which are relatively resistant to change (e.g. those formed a long time ago, such as 'my early childhood');

broad constructs, which can be widely applied (e.g. 'All pop music is awful');

constricted constructs, which can only be applied narrowly (e.g. 'The only subject I like is English');

core constructs, which refer to ourselves and maintain our identity;

tight constructs, which are prone to collapse altogether if you tinker with them, like scientific laws;

loose constructs, which vary dependent upon the situation (e.g. 'A summer day can be wet or dry').

Obviously, some constructs can belong to more than one category, as for example many of our core constructs.

Kelly considers that personality problems arise when an individual's constructs are inadequate to help him predict what is going to happen next. *This* is the reason, says Kelly, why it is so important to treat children with consistency. If we fail to do so, their constructs become a confused and contradictory mess, and it is no wonder that they suffer from incongruence. What kind of construct can a child have of 'teacher', or of 'justice', or of 'honesty', or of 'trust', or of any of these things, if one day his teacher praises him, the next punishes him, and the next ignores him for behaviour which, in his own eyes, does not really vary that much? The world becomes as confusing for him as it would for us if one day potatoes satisfied us and the next made us hungry.

Kelly expresses impatience with the fact that modern psychology has tended to fragment itself into separate topics such as 'learning', 'motivation' and 'memory'. This is contrary, he claims, to the humanistic view that man should be treated as a person. Our mental life is not broken up into these various categories. We function, normally at least, as a psychological unit. One of the values of construct theory, he claims, is that it allows psychology to avoid this fragmentation. The individual's behaviour at any one time is largely a matter of the constructs he has about the task in hand. Kelly even doubts whether, in education, we have served a useful purpose by taking something such as 'intelligence' and focusing so much attention on it out of the context of the rest of the child's behaviour.

As already intimated, if the child is labelled 'intelligent', this will inevitably bias the construct that the teacher holds of him. Research such as that reviewed by Delamont (1984) shows clearly the extent to which teacher behaviours (influenced in turn by the constructs which teachers hold of their children and of their own educational role) can influence child behaviours. Thus if, for example, a teacher has the construct that one child is particularly intelligent, her behaviour towards him is likely to reflect the fact. This is of course the well known 'halo effect', and it works equally effectively in reverse, as any child who has tried to live down a bad classroom reputation well knows.

Instead, Kelly claims that our constructs of children should be as holistic as possible. The teacher should get to know the whole child, which means studying the range of the child's psychological experience, and trying to learn as much as she can about the constructs which the child has formed to deal with life. Where these are inappropriate, we should help him to change them, using the kind of empathic understanding and positive regard advocated by Rogers. Where the child does not get help of this kind, he develops the ego-defence mechanisms isolated by Freud, particularly if it is his core constructs that are faulty.

Kelly even suggests that construct theory can help us to understand a child's cognitive development. Though he has no real quarrel with the work of Piaget, he considers that the developmental stages which Piaget has isolated in the child's cognitive growth may be owing as much to the fact that children accumulate more constructs with the passage of time as to the fact that intellectual processes are dependent upon physiological maturation. As the child accumulates constructs, more and more pieces of the intellectual jigsaw fall into place, and he gets a more accurate picture of how the world really works. Assuming that he experiences consistency and emotional support from his environment, the child builds up constructs that possess what Kelly calls a *wide range of convenience*, constructs that can be used to interpret accurately and efficiently a large repertory of situations, and thus make the world appear a less uncertain and threatening place.

Kelly's method for examining the individual's construct system is more time-consuming than Q-sorting or the Semantic Differential (see chapter 4), but it elicits information in a much more structured and more searching way. It consists basically of establishing the similarities and dissimilarities which the individual sees between the people and things in his life. We can explain it best by taking a specific example. Suppose we wanted to examine a child's constructs about 'people important to me'. We start by asking him to list these people, writing each name down on a separate card as he gives it to us. We then take three of the cards at random – let's say 'mother', 'father' and 'teacher' – and ask the child to tell us any way in which two of them are alike and different from the third. He might tell us that mother and teacher are strict, and father is not. We next get him to apply this strict–lenient distinction (or construct, since that is what it is) to each of the other people whose names he has given us (is grandad strict? is his best friend strict?), before we return these cards to the pile, draw another three at random, and try again. This time he may tell us that father and uncle are fun, but that the head teacher isn't. Once more this distinction is applied to all the other people, the cards returned to the pile, and the process repeated again. In fact we go on repeating the process until the child has exhausted all the differences and similarities between the important people in his life (perhaps surprisingly, experience shows that, whatever the area we are investigating, usually no more than thirty or so of these differences and similarities emerge, and often there are far fewer).

This method is known as *repertory-grid technique* (see, for instance, Fransella and Bannister 1977), because we display our results in the form of a grid, with names across the top and distinctions (constructs) down the side, and a 1 or a 0 in each cell of the grid (figure 3) depending upon a person's rating on the construct concerned (e.g. mother and teacher would rate 1 on strictness, father 0). The finished grid is a representation of the child's 'people important to me' constructs. (We can carry out the same exercise with other areas of the child's life, such as important events, the school curriculum, and so on.) Analysis of the grids shows us the nature and complexity of a child's constructs. For example, what sort of constructs seem to characterise the important people in his life? Warm, accepting constructs, or cold rejecting ones? Do these constructs cover a broad range, such as 'clever', 'interesting', 'sporting', or are they restricted to mundane things? Do the people in his life generally seem strong and effective and good role models, or are they weak and negative? And who seems to be like whom? Is father like the other members of the family on most things, or is he more like remoter people? Is there a polarisation into males and females? Into old and young?

Although a repertory grid requires care in its compilation and in its interpretation, there are potentially few limits to the kind of information that it can provide. And numerous variants of this basic grid have also been devised (see, for instance, Fransella 1981). Hinkle (1965) has developed the *implications grid* which compares constructs rather than people or events, and enables us to establish, for example, what the construct 'successful' means to the child (perhaps 'hard working', 'honest', 'like me', or mayby 'lucky', 'stuck up', 'not like me'). Ravenette (1975) has devised a *situations grid*, of particular value for use with children, which employs pictures rather than words.

	Mother	Teacher	Father	Uncle	Head teacher	Grandfather	Aunt	Friend	etc.
Strict	1	1	0	?	?	?	?	?	
Fun	?	?	1	1	0	?	?	?	
etc.									

Figure 3

To Kelly, the overriding virtue of repertory-grid technique is that it actually *involves* the person who is being tested. He is asked direct questions about the important things in his life, and we actually give him credit for knowing the answers. In this it differs from so many other psychological techniques (e.g. projective techniques, and the behaviouristic methods that we shall be looking at in chapter 8), which maintain an elaborate mystique, or which frequently make the assumption that the psychologist knows more about a person than the person knows about himself. They obey, in fact, what Kelly called his *first principle*: that is that, if you really want to know what is wrong with people, you should try asking them; 'they might just be able to tell you' (Kelly 1955).

Using repertory grids

To take an example of how a grid might be used with a child in school, let us suppose that we are working with a backward reader and decide to construct a grid to establish his construct of 'reading' and thus his motivation for wanting to improve reading efficiency. Typically, we might find that his construct is a very limited one indeed, and goes a long way towards explaining why he has little real incentive for improving. The repertory grid shows that he sees reading as 'boring', as 'unlike my other interests', as a pastime for 'old' and 'dull' people, as identified with 'failure' and so on. Once this sorry picture has emerged, it can be discussed with the child and its inhibiting nature made apparent. We can then invite the child to work through the grid again, this time identifying all the things that would make him take an interest in reading. Reading, it seems, would be fun for him if it were 'exciting', if it 'helped with other interests', if it were identified with 'success', and the like. The teacher's task now becomes to demonstrate to the child, by suitable choice of reading-materials, by setting the right level of difficulty, by relating reading to his hobbies, and so on, that reading can indeed fit closely into the 'interest in reading' construct that he has already identified.

At the personality level (though Kelly would not have isolated such things as reading-skills from personality; success or failure in reading is likely to have a profound effect upon personality, particularly in such areas as self-esteem), grids can be used extensively to explore virtually all aspects of the way in which we experience ourselves. For example, we can construct grids on 'myself', on 'my emotions', on 'how others see me', on 'my goals in life', and on anything else you care to mention. Nor does it end there. Thomas and Harri-Augstein (1985) list over 200 areas of personal experiencing over and above straightforward investigations into personality that they have explored in recent research. These range from 'jobs I'd like to do' to 'methods I found successful in breaking habits', from 'families I know' to 'outcomes from listening to a lecture', and from 'responses to personal crises' to 'prayer meetings'. One of the most important aspects of their work is that they have developed programmes which allow grids to be constructed with the use of the computer, enabling children and adults to work on their own with grid material, exploring their own inner world of fears and beliefs and feelings, and experimenting with the way in which this inner world might be changed as a consequence of re-sorting the constructs thus revealed. Work of this kind has implications for all aspects of human learning, and not just for those aspects that have to do with personality. With the universal presence of computers in schools, teachers now have at their command a powerful medium for helping children's personal and academic development, and for taking increasing personal responsibility for this development.

Essentially what the repertory grid helps us to do is to explore the inner world in a way which is beyond the measuring-techniques of the trait theorists. It thus allows psychologists to use what is called the introspective method (inviting people to introspect about their own states of mind), a method which had for long fallen into disrepute in psychology because it was held to be far too subjective and imprecise. Above all it allows us to look at the constantly changing state of our own mental lives and of the mental lives of others, to view the flux of our personalities and to see where the need and the opportunities for personal change lie. Two repertory grids referring to the same topic can be taken with the same person only days apart and show quite remarkable alterations or developments in the way in which the topics are construed. Thus, on the topic of 'self', for example, a student's constructs in the anxious days before a major examination may be very markedly different from the constructs that emerge after the successful outcome, as indeed may be the case for his constructs on a wide range of things that at first and even second sight appear to have very little to do with the examination itself. It is perhaps not for nothing that Thomas and Harri-Augstein, discussing the way in which repertory-grid technique has made the inner psychological world accessible, suggest that in the future the technique may be seen as marking a 'watershed in social sciences comparable to Copernicus and the telescope in natural science'.

Other state-based theorists

A state-based approach rather different from that of Kelly is exemplified by the work of Michael Apter (1982). Apter diverges from Kelly in that, although he sees personality as made up of states rather than traits, he argues that amongst these shifting, fluctuating states we can nevertheless identify certain dimensions. These are not analogous to the dimensions used in trait theory, upon which the individual has a fixed position, but are dimensions along which the individual moves ('reverses') in accordance with his state at the time. Apter suggests the existence of a range of these dimensions, but space only allows us to look at the best known, namely the *telic–paratelic* dimension. When at the telic end of the dimension, the individual tackles life purposefully, producing goal-directed behaviour in which the activities of the moment (the means) are subservient to the ultimate purpose (the ends). In the paratelic state, by contrast, the activities of the moment are all-important, and the ends, if any, are simply an excuse for engaging in these activities. Thus, for example, one might swim to save one's life (in which case one's swimming would be undertaken in the telic state) or purely for pleasure (in which case it would be undertaken in the paratelic state).

Some individuals may prefer to be in the telic state for much of the time, while others may prefer to be in the paratelic (and these preferences can be assessed by a questionnaire known as the Telic Dominance Scale), but most people are able to reverse between the two states dependent upon the demands of the moment. We may, for instance, be in the telic state when at work (seeing the job simply as a way of making an honest living) and in the paratelic state when out for a Saturday-morning stroll (seeing the goal of getting to the shops to buy a newspaper simply as a useful excuse for the pleasure of stretching our legs).

At school level, the telic–paratelic dimension is of considerable importance. Some children appear to move readily into the telic state, working hard even at relatively tedious work since this will help them through an examination, say, while others move more readily into the paratelic and find it more difficult to take anything very seriously. Some children can be telic or paratelic as the occasion demands, while others find it harder to reverse between the two states as necessary. Similarly, some teachers are determinedly telic and find it difficult to be paratelic in school or to relate to paratelic behaviour in children, while other teachers may prefer to be paratelic and in consequence may find problems with those parts of their job that require telic behaviours.

Many classroom confrontations will obviously occur when a telic-minded teacher tries to work with a paratelic-minded class, with both parties unable to reverse sufficiently freely between the two states. Since Apter argues that normally no one is permanently located at either extreme end of the telic–paratelic dimension, the teacher should learn to identify which state is required in any particular task from a child, and then help the latter move into this state and recognise its existence in himself. Similarly, the teacher should learn how best to move into this state for his own part.

Apter's model also stretches to the counselling of children with personality problems. For example, our treatment of a child who steals for telic reasons (to obtain money for a particular purpose) may be different from that of a child who steals in the paratelic state (simply for excitement). Similarly, a child playing truant through school phobia (and therefore in the telic state) will require different forms of counselling from the child who plays truant for the sheer fun of it (and who is therefore in the paratelic state), just as the child who bullies others to gain attention (telic state) is a different kind of problem from the child who bullies because he enjoys bullying (paratelic state).

From the teacher's point of view, we must repeat again that a key aspect of the state-based approach is that it allows for the possibility of producing desirable changes in personality, even in the short term. If personality does indeed fluctuate from day to day and even from hour to hour, then this allows us scope to influence such fluctuations. Bloom (1983) therefore suggests that the teacher should examine each learning-task offered to children and determine in advance the *affective entry behaviours* (i.e. the personality states) which the child should manifest at the beginning of the task if his chances of success are to be optimised. He may perhaps need to be in the telic state defined by Apter, or need to try and cultivate a degree of introversion, or need to stop worrying too much about outcomes, or whatever. One way of formalising our thinking about affective entry behaviours proposed by Bloom is that we should study the child's affect towards, respectively, self, school and the subject to be learnt. Is the child's affect (i.e. the whole range of his emotions, attitudes, concepts, and so on) towards himself characterised by self-esteem and confidence, for example? Is his affect towards school a positive one and does he identify with the values and aims of the school and of his teacher? Does he see the subject to be learnt as a useful and interesting one?

If the answers to questions such as these are in the negative, Bloom argues, the teacher can take steps to put things right. Without these steps, the child's chances of success are severely limited. His self-esteem and confidence can be quickly enhanced for instance by giving him short preliminary tasks which allow him to experience success. His affect towards school and teacher can be immediately helped if the teacher adopts a friendly and humorous manner, while his affect towards the subject can be improved if that subject is presented in a way which at once captures interest. Each of these interventions by the teacher is designed to produce quick changes in the child's affects. Those who doubt the possibility of such changes may like to reflect how we warm immediately towards someone who gives us a friendly smile, how our interest is at once captured by a film or television programme that opens with an action sequence or by setting us an immediate puzzle, and how our confidence is straightaway boosted in any task if we find ourselves operating successfully at it.

Just as the teacher can produce these changes in her children, so she can produce them in herself. Rather than discuss the teacher's personality in terms of supposedly enduring traits such as extroversion and introversion, Bloom considers that once again we should simply think in terms of affective entry behaviours. What affective behaviours does the teacher need at the beginning of a lesson if that lesson is to be a success? Usually, for example, she will need a positive attitude towards her children and towards their learning-potential, and a positive attitude towards her teaching-subject and towards her ability at putting it across. If she has experienced past failure, then she should start the lesson with activities that she knows will be effective, and should allow her own confidence and her attitude towards the children to be enhanced as she observes the improved standards being obtained.

Emotional states

The discussion of emotions is best carried out within the context of the state-based approach, since the very fact that traditionally we use the word 'states' to refer to emotions indicates that we recognise their transitory nature. Pleasant or unpleasant, emotions come and go, and it is doubtful indeed whether certain high-arousal emotional states (anger, excitement, fear) could be sustained by most people for any length of time without having a deleterious effect upon both physical and psychological health. Nevertheless, some people appear much more prone to experiencing emotions than do others (in fact we refer to them as 'very emotional'), though they may be selective in the emotions they experience. That is, they may frequently experience fear or sorrow, but rarely anger or jealousy, or frequently experience joy but rarely sadness.

One of the difficulties psychologists face when exploring emotions is that they are highly subjective states. Physiologically, both anger and sexual arousal might appear to be the same things (increased heart rate and blood pressure, rise in body temperature, burn-up of nervous energy, and so on), but it hardly needs saying that to the person experiencing the emotions concerned they could hardly seem more different. Thus simply to take readings of physiological arousal tells us very little about the way a particular emotion *feels* to the person who is going through it. Indeed, even what seems to be the same emotion (the high arousal associated with risk-taking, for example, or with a horror film) may be experienced quite differently by two people. For one person the emotion is experienced as pleasurable and is in consequence sought after, while to the other it is upsetting and something very much to be avoided. This difficulty in assessing emotions objectively means that we often simply have to rely upon what people tell us about themselves, and, as indicated earlier, this kind of introspection is unacceptable to many psychologists on grounds of imprecision.

Trait theorists such as Eysenck suggest that the best way to conceptualise emotions is to see them as physiological states mediated by the autonomic nervous system – that is, to see them as physical experiences set off by the autonomic nervous system (that part of the nervous system which normally functions independently of our conscious control), and which are perceived by the experiencer as either pleasant or unpleasant. As life goes on we come to learn which environmental stimuli trigger off pleasant states and which trigger off unpleasant, and we generally seek out the former and avoid the latter. Recently Gray (1985) has put forward a model which seeks to show how an emotion such as anxiety can be directly related to changes in brain chemistry associated with autonomic functioning. Some individuals (perhaps innately) are more likely to experience these changes, and therefore to become anxious, in the face of threats and the like from the outside world, and therefore could be described in layman's language as anxiety-prone, or to have an anxiety trait and therefore to score above average on anxiety measures such as Eysenck's N scale (see chapter 6).

To the state theorist, however, to say that someone is anxiety-prone is relatively unhelpful. What is of far greater importance is what makes a particular person anxious, how he experiences his anxiety (as something daunting and unpleasant, for example, or as a useful stimulus towards getting work done or problems solved), and what kind of strategies he develops for dealing with or avoiding anxiety. For all we know, the world may be full of people who rarely experience anxiety because they have learnt how to handle or to avoid it. Such people might not score much higher on Eysenck's N dimension than do those people who naturally rarely feel anxious about things, yet in a psychological sense they are significantly different, as might become apparent if we asked them for instance to take over the job of teaching other people how to handle their 'nerves'.

At the classroom level, clearly the teacher's main interest is to observe what causes emotional states in particular children and how they try and deal with them, rather than to assign trait labels (such as 'John is timid', 'Karen has a temper', 'Paul is carefree', 'Sandra is jealous', 'Betty is affectionate'). In this sense, then, the state-based approach is likely to be more helpful. The same is true when it comes to 'moods', which are indefinite things but which seem to be emotional states persisting over a rather longer period of time, including perhaps the aftermath of an emotional state when we no longer feel the emotion quite so keenly but still allow the memory of it to colour our thinking and our responses to the people and events around us.

In spite of their probable link with in-born temperament (the 'difficult' children we looked at in chapter 1 in connection with the work of Thomas, Chess and Birch, for example, were noted as having a 'crankiness' of mood from the early weeks of life on), there is little doubt that emotions and moods are also very much under environmental influence. Individuals with a secure and loving home, who have satisfactory levels of self-esteem and who are used to the experience of success are more likely to be optimistic and happy than are individuals who come from difficult and stressful backgrounds. Children who are able to discuss their problems freely and positively with their parents are less likely to engage in sullen brooding than children who are the victims of unfair and unsympathetic homes. Children who are taught a sensible and humane moral code are less likely to be tortured by feelings of guilt and inadequacy than children expected to adhere to impossibly rigid and arbitrary standards.

As in the home, so in the school. Children who are faced with unfairness, frustrations and constant failure are far more likely to be hostile and disruptive than children who work with teachers who are supportive, consistent and realistic. Children from schools with a plethora of seemingly meaningless and petty rules, or with timetables that contain little variety or practical work, are far more likely to be rebellious than children from schools which are sensitive to their needs and more democratic and flexible in approach. Children who can find no one on the staff ready to listen to their problems and provide the right help and guidance are far more likely to take these problems out on others (by attention-seeking behaviour, for example, or aggression) than children who know where to turn in times of difficulty.

These points are particularly true in adolescence, when children are facing the various physical and emotional upheavals of puberty and of the transition into adult life. Schools who fail to understand the nature of the search for identity (see chapter 2) at this stage, and who fail to provide an education which is seen by the children concerned to be relevant to their present and future needs, can hardly expect to encourage the co-operative and positive moods needed if educational progress is to be made. But, whether it be at adolescence or at earlier stages of school life, it is vital that teachers do everything feasible to monitor children's emotional states. Much of this monitoring is straightforward and easy enough. It may be noted, for example, that a class is always in a restless mood when they come from an active lesson such as games or physical education to more sedentary work in the classroom, or when they come from working with another teacher, or when it nears the end of the week. Similarly, certain individuals may appear particularly excitable at certain identifiable times (perhaps the lesson before a television programme), or particularly difficult at others. Children from unsatisfactory homes may be extra troublesome on Monday mornings, after spending the weekend at close quarters with their families, while children having problems with their schoolwork may be especially disruptive during lessons where they feel their poor progress will be contrasted in public ways with the progress of their more successful classmates.

In all these instances, the teacher can take steps, in consultation where appropriate with colleagues, either to alter the circumstances which lead to problems, or to provide the children concerned with extra support. Sudden changes in mood in children who have hitherto been sunny and co-operative in behaviour should also be identified and watched carefully until the causes (whether at home or school) have been discovered. Children with emotional problems, whatever the reason, should be helped through counselling to discuss their difficulties and to understand that we can gain gradual control over our emotions, not through rigid self-discipline and repression but through the ability to recognise more clearly the nature of the emotion, what sparks it off, and what its consequences are for both self and others (see, for instance, Fontana 1985). The more familiar we become with our emotions, the less we feel ourselves to be in their power. This entails not guilt or self-recriminations when we become involved in undesirable emotions, but instead a sensible and objective appraisal of what is happening to us and why. With patience and goodwill on the part of both teacher and child, the education of moods and the emotions can become a part of the whole process of school-based learning.

Criticisms of the state-based approach

The state-based approach attracts some of the criticisms levelled at humanistic psychology (see chapter 4): namely, that it is imprecise and too dependent upon the individual's own ability to describe his psychological states to us. While Kelly's first principle (if you want to know what's wrong with people try asking them; 'they might just be able to tell you') is laudable enough, there may be numerous occasions when people might just *not* be able to tell us what is wrong with them. These criticisms have some justification, but evidence is increasing that the results yielded by repertory grids provide us with information that is impressively accurate. In addition to the successful use of grids in those areas instanced earlier in the chapter, Fransella (1981) reviews results which show that even with thought-disordered subjects such as schizophrenics (see chapter 11) grids can produce information revealing enough to be of great practical benefit in devising and monitoring treatment. At school level, enough has already been said to show how grids can be used, with or without the aid of the computer, to help not only the teacher's understanding of the child but also the child's understanding of himself.

Other state-based theorists discussed in this chapter, such as Apter and Bloom, have also produced impressive evidence to show how their own work can be used to help children in key areas such as learning, counselling and self-development. As to whether the personality is better conceived in terms of a set of persisting traits or in terms of a set of shifting and flowing states, the reader must in the end, as already indicated, judge for himself. It may be of interest to learn that in the East, and in the philosophical and psychological systems associated with vast and profound areas of thought such as Hinduism and Buddhism, it has unquestionably been accepted for thousands of years that the state-based explanation is the correct one. More, it has been accepted that the notion of enduring personality traits is a dangerous delusion, and a major obstacle on the road to psychological and spiritual development. There are interesting parallels here with Thomas and Harri-Augstein (1985), whose work within the context of the repertory grid suggests to them that it is the myth of a static mind that is the 'fundamental flaw in any approach to learning' and which underpins 'misguided fixed measures' of personality (and, incidentally, of intelligence and aptitude to). Trait theorists reply, not surprisingly, that an approach of this kind robs us of the chance for seeking common personality principles among the population at large, since of necessity it places the major emphasis upon working with individuals. It also robs psychology of the chance of becoming a science, if by 'science' we mean a subject that deals with persistent and consistent data. And there, regrettably, we must leave a debate that is likely to be perhaps the major issue in personality studies for some years to come. Readers wishing to pursue it further are referred to Fontana (1983).

8

Behaviourism and Personality

We must now look at the contributions that the last of the main forces in psychology, behaviourism, has made to the study of personality (see Fontana 1984 for a review of behaviourism and education). It claims to be the most objective and scientific approach, since it concerns itself not with what people have to tell you about their own states of mind, but with what they actually *do* (i.e. with their behaviour). It rejects all reference to the sort of mechanisms that psychoanalysis and humanistic psychology see as underlying personality, and has shown no particular enthusiasm even for such devices as trait measurement. The trouble with all these things, say the behaviourists, is that they rely largely upon pure speculation. Nobody can observe the unconscious at work (or even test its workings, as we can with something like remembering), and no one knows for sure whether traits amount to much more than scores on a personality inventory.

On the other hand, under controlled laboratory conditions at least, we can all agree on a man's (or an animal's) behaviour. Does he respond quickly to a particular stimulus, or does he take a long time? Do his physiological responses (raised heart rate, blood pressure, and so on) show him to be tense and angry, or calm and relaxed? Does he take three tries before he picks up a simple learning-task, or does he take four or five? It is these things, say the behaviourists, that turn psychology into a science, not the speculations of men such Freud and Maslow. And of course, as to Kelly's first principle that someone with personality problems might just know what is wrong with himself (see chapter 7), they would answer that we have no way of knowing whether he does or not until we have observed his behaviour carefully enough.

Behaviourism was first proposed by the American psychologist J. B. Watson in 1913, and has enjoyed great popularity in the USA and, to a somewhat lesser extent, Europe. It refers to units of behaviour as *responses*, and sees these as consisting partly of innate reflexes (e.g. sucking, crying), but mostly of learnt reactions. It is this stress upon learning that causes behaviourism to be known by its alternative title of *learning-theory*. To understand man, say the behaviourists, one has to study the way in which he acquires his repertory of responses. That is all.

Learning-theory is much too extensive to be discussed fully here (see Bigge 1982). We shall simply look at its main two subdivisions, *classical conditioning* and *operant conditioning*.

Classical conditioning

Classical conditioning, first discovered by the Russian physiologist Ivan Pavlov (1839–1936), occurs when an innate reflex (called an unconditioned response, or UR) becomes elicited not just by its natural or unconditioned stimulus (US) but by an unnatural stimulus (a conditioned stimulus, or CS) as well. This happens if the CS and the US occur close together frequently. Thus if a light is flashed (CS) every time we get an electric shock (US), the wince (UR) normally elicited by the shock in time becomes elicited by the light alone. The wince is now called a *conditioned response*.

Pavlov believed that the whole of the complex activity of man is simply a collection of conditioned responses. The baby's love for his mother, for example, would thus be explained by the fact that the mother is present as a CS every time the baby receives his milk (US). Over a period of time, the pleasure which is the UR to the milk becomes elicited as a conditioned response (CR) by the mother as well, even when it is not feeding-time. Evidence that stimulus-response bonds, as they are called, of this kind can be set up was allegedly produced by Watson himself (Watson and Rayner 1919), who found that the natural fear which a baby boy called Albert had for loud noises appeared to become associated as well with the previously innocuous stimulus of a white rat, if rat and noise were produced together often enough. Through what Watson called *stimulus generalisation*, it was then found that Albert had also apparently become afraid of anything that looked like a white rat, such as a white rabbit or even Watson himself in a long white Santa Claus beard.

Subsequently doubts have been expressed about these findings, and attempts to replicate them have met with very mixed results. It is also now known that, although some behaviour can be explained through classical conditioning, it is inadequate as an explanation of all behaviour. The learning which it accounts for seems to be largely confined to responses which occur in the autonomic nervous system (i.e. to involuntary rather than to consciously mediated responses), and, in any case, conditioned responses tend to weaken and disappear (become extinct) as soon as the US and the CS finally cease to occur together. Behaviourism, nowadays, tends therefore to pay much more attention to operant conditioning.

Operant conditioning

Operant conditioning differs from classical conditioning chiefly in that, instead of concentrating upon the stimulus which *precedes* a response, it concentrates upon the consequences that follow *after* the response. Operant-conditioning theory holds that if a response has pleasant consequences (is 'rewarded' or 'reinforced') it tends to be repeated; if it has unpleasant consequences (is 'punished' in some way) it tends not to be. This principle was originally stated, at somewhat greater length, by one of the pioneers of behaviourism, the American psychologist E. L. Thorndike (1874–1949) in his 'Law of Effect', but it is now particularly associated with the work of perhaps the best known of all American psychologists, B. F. Skinner (b. 1904).

Skinner, in a number of publications (e.g. 1974), takes up Thorndike's view that, since human behaviour most frequently occurs in the absence of any precedent stimulus, classical conditioning, even if it were not subject to extinction and covered learning in the central nervous system as well as in the autonomic, could not explain most of human behaviour. He also maintains that we should give up the idea that behaviour is prompted by instincts, needs or drives such as those suggested by the psychoanalysts or the humanists. Instead, we should 'shift to the environment a causal role previously assigned to a person's feelings, states of mind, purposes, or other attributes' (1972). This does not mean that Skinner rejects the idea of innate differences. People differ from each other in their physiological endowments, and therefore must differ from each other in the level of the responses which they make to the environment. What he does reject is the idea that man's habits, his likes and dislikes, his beliefs, his moral judgements – in sum, his personality – is anything more than a set of learned responses to the particular environmental circumstances he has encountered during his life to date. Thus the belief that man has free will, or autonomy, or control over his individual destiny, is an illusion.

Over the last forty years, Skinner has amassed a great deal of evidence, working with both men and with animals, in support of this view. The details of this evidence belong more to a book on learning than to one on personality, but we can see how they can be applied to personality if we take the example of a child who is consistently misbehaving in class. Skinner would say that the child is misbehaving not because he 'feels' like it (i.e. as the result of a freely taken decision), but because of the experiences that he has had in life so far. These experiences have rewarded (reinforced) his disruptive behaviour, have stamped it in and made it a part of his personality. He may be a child with an unstimulating home background, who has tended only to be reinforced with adult attention when he behaves badly. Good behaviour goes unnoticed, and therefore has tended to disappear from his behavioural repertoire. Or he may be a friendless child, who is only rewarded with the approval of his peers when he enlivens things by cheeking the teacher. Or he may be a child who is backward in class and who is largely ignored by the teacher unless he becomes disruptive.

If we take the opposite example of a child who behaves well, Skinner would say that this good behaviour is a result of the frequent and sympathetic adult attention with which such behaviour has been reinforced at home. Where we have a well-behaved child who, for example, becomes difficult on the birth of a baby sibling, Skinner would deny that this has anything to do with regression (chapter 3) and would say it is simply because the mother is now too busy to notice him when he is good, and only turns her attention to him when he does something wrong.

Note that what Skinner is saying here is that the very *fact* of adult attention can be rewarding to a child, even though it be angry attention. Adults often assume that simply because they are speaking crossly to a child he is actually experiencing punishment, whereas in truth the real punishment might be to ignore him altogether. By speaking crossly to him, one is at least acknowledging his existence, and, by showing him that he is important enough to make adults angry, one is demonstrating that he has power over the immediate environment. We shall return to this point later in the chapter, but what Skinner is in effect saying is that often we make children's behaviour worse by inadvertently reinforcing it when we imagine ourselves to be doing the opposite.

It can probably be deduced from what we have said already that Skinner's attitude to psychoanalysis and humanistic psychology is a very antagonistic one. He sees no reason for postulating the existence of id, ego or super-ego, or meta needs, or ego-defence mechanisms, or for the various processes that psychoanalysts and humanistic psychologists advance to account for the existence of neuroses. People become neurotic, Skinner argues, because their environment makes them so – in particular, through reinforcing them in a haphazard and unpredictable way, and by handing out harsh punishments. It is quite possible to make a laboratory animal 'neurotic' by this kind of treatment, and no one suggests that laboratory animals have id, ego and super-ego.

Skinner is very much less at odds with Eysenck and with the trait-based approach to personality than he is with the psychoanalysts and humanists (and indeed Eysenck is very much less at odds with Skinner). He would accept Eysenck's attempt to relate the personality to such physiological systems as the hypothalamus and the reticular formation areas of the brain. He would also accept Eysenck's view that a large percentage of attributes such as anxiety and introversion may be inherited, if by inherited we mean that some people develop the conditioned responses that are described as 'anxiety' and 'introversion' more readily than do others.

Of course, Skinner does not pretend that it is always possible to point to the precise cause in a person's environment of each item of his present behaviour. The consequences of a particular learning-experience, especially in a complex society such as ours, are often long delayed. But the rule remains that all behaviour is caused. Thus, when we observe an activity that seems to us to be spontaneous and creative, we are simply witnessing the consequences of a piece of experience that may have taken place much earlier. 'Consequences', says Skinner (1972), 'take over a role previously assigned to an antecedent creative mind.' Embedded in this line of reasoning is Skinner's emphasis upon *performance* as well as upon learning. We are learning new things all the time, but this learning may not be very apparent in our performance until it is suddenly reinforced by our environment. Thus a child may learn to discriminate between musical notes, but show little sign of this skill until he is suddenly reinforced by teacher approval when he starts taking music lessons.

Skinner recognises the existence of both primary and secondary reinforcers. The former (e.g. food, warmth, shelter) have intrinsic value, the latter (e.g. money) have not, but have become desirable through their association with the former. In our complex society, a great deal of social behaviour is the result of secondary reinforcement. Since a school is a particularly artificial environment, in which children have to learn in a few years information that has taken centuries of research and discovery, Skinner accepts that it cannot help but rely upon secondary reinforcement (such as teacher approval, good grades, examination success). Usually these secondary reinforcers are built into what Skinner calls 'chains', with each reinforcer associated with the next and so on back to a primary reinforcer. Thus a child values good marks (secondary reinforcer) because they are associated with parental approval (secondary reinforcer), which is associated with improved creature comforts (primary reinforcer). As might be predicted from his extreme environmental viewpoint, Skinner places great emphasis upon the importance of education, and deplores the fact that, partly through teachers' misapplication of reinforcers, it is generally so inefficient.

We shall be returning shortly to some of the things that Skinner claims can be done to render education more efficient, but first we'll look at another set of learning-theories, somewhat related to operant conditioning by virtue of their similar emphasis upon the environment – namely, social-learning theories.

Social-learning theories

Social-learning theories are associated particularly with the work of Albert Bandura (b. 1925). Bandura has been much influenced by the behaviourists, but he differs from them in insisting that much behaviour takes place in the absence of any kind of reinforcement at all. The child, he claims, has an innate propensity for copying the behaviour of others, even when he receives no reward for doing so. Much learning, therefore, takes place by *imitation* (or *modelling*). It is strange that before the work of Bandura and of other social-learning theorists, psychologists had tended to neglect imitation as an important element in shaping human behaviour.

Imitation, Bandura claims (e.g. 1969), explains both broad cultural movements (fashions, fads, mass hysteria, and so on) and the individual socialisation of the child. The child's personality is, therefore, largely an imitation, within the limits laid down by innate differences, of those around him. In a sense, Bandura helps span a small part of the gap between the behaviourists and the psychoanalysts, since he would accept the latter's emphasis upon the child's acquisition of role behaviour from his parents, though he has shown little enthusiasm for the idea of various systems within the personality, or for meta needs. As for self-actualisation, Bandura would claim that the child's basic need to copy those around him is sufficient explanation of the origin of many of the goals and aims that he develops in life.

Bandura's emphasis upon the possibility of learning taking place in the absence of reinforcement does not mean that he sees the latter as unimportant. A child is more likely to imitate a model who is being rewarded for his actions than one who is being punished, and, once having imitated his behaviour, this imitation is more likely to persist if it is rewarded in its own turn. Bandura also accepts Skinner's distinction between learning and performance. A child need not necessarily *perform* the actions of another at the moment he is learning them. He can store up these actions mentally and produce them at an appropriate time later on, as when a boy watches a cowboy film and next day at school acts out the role of the hero.

Bandura also considers that, the more prestigious the model, the more likely the child will be to imitate his behaviour (hence violence on the football field by a star player is more likely to spread to the watching crowd than violence by a lesser-known one). Since this imitation goes on in the absence of rewards and punishments, this means that the child may well be learning many things from a prestigious model such as his teacher which the model herself has no idea she is teaching. This is particularly true of emotions. The child may have all kinds of emotional behaviour modelled unwittingly for him by the teacher, such as sympathy towards those in difficulties, or impatience and anger. Bandura has made a special study of aggression, which he feels lends itself especially well to a social learning-theory interpretation. In a number of research studies (see Bandura 1973 for a summary), he has shown that children who witness adult aggression are much more likely to behave aggressively themselves than are children who do not. It is as if the adult aggression sanctions similar behaviour in children. And, of course, if the children find that this aggression pays off in helping them to get their own way, then it may become an established part of their behaviour.

Innate differences and the child's own previous experiences will obviously affect the extent to which social learning takes place. Jakubczak and Walters (1959) show that dependent children imitate prestige figures more readily than do those who are less dependent, and that timid or anxious children take over fearful responses vicariously more frequently than do secure and confident ones. Similarly, children who have learnt to respond warmly to teachers in the past will be far readier to take them as models in the present, while someone who has learnt, for instance, to despise the opposite sex, will be less likely to accept a member of that sex as a model than will someone who has learnt to respect it. Similarly again, a child who has seen someone behaving ineffectually in the past, or receiving frequent punishment, will be less likely to accept that person as a model than he will be to accept someone who has been behaving with success.

In the next section we shall be looking at some of the practical applications of Bandura's theories for the teacher, together with the application of those of Skinner.

Techniques for modifying children's behaviour

If, as the behaviourists believe, personality problems such as neuroticism or maladjustment are simply caused by the wrong kinds of stimulus-response bonds or by the wrong kinds of reinforcement, it follows that, if we want to cure people of these problems, all we have to do is to break these bonds or to reverse this reinforcement. This, indeed, is the principle behind *behaviour therapy*, which is the behaviouristic equivalent of psychoanalysis or Rogerian therapy. It has the advantage of extreme simplicity, and, in certain circumstances at least, it seems to work. To see how it does, perhaps we could first go back to Watson's experiment with little Albert. If we are indeed able to condition Albert to feel fear for the white rat by associating it with the unpleasant stimulus of the loud noise, we can in theory remove this fear (in other words, *desensitise* Albert) by now associating the white rat with something pleasant. This means presenting the rat to Albert along with something of which he is very fond, say jelly. Each time Albert sees the rat, he gets his plate of jelly. This has to be done discreetly, with a respectable distance at first between the rat and Albert while he eats his jelly, otherwise his aversion for the rat could just end up by being associated with the jelly.

Similarly, by *aversion* therapy, it is possible to turn somebody against something (a bad habit, a deviant activity), just as Albert was apparently turned against the rat in the first place, by pairing it with something unpleasant. Thus, for example, a smoker can be given an electric shock every time he opens his cagarette packet, or a finger-nail biter can have his nails coated with a foul tasting substance.

Desensitisation and aversion therapy have been used extensively to treat a wide range of anxieties, phobias and deviances. It will be noted that no time is wasted probing the subject's previous experience to find the exact situation that gave rise to the unwanted behaviour. Nor is this behaviour seen as a symptom of some deeper, unconscious malaise. The symptom and the anxiety, or phobia or whatever it happens to be, are seen as essentially the same thing, with the cure of the former necessarily also curing the latter.

Desensitisation and aversion therapy are based, of course, on classical-conditioning techniques. The operant-conditioning approach to behaviour therapy is somewhat broader. It focuses upon consistently reinforcing the wanted behaviour, while at the same time, if possible, withholding reinforcement from the unwanted. Thus, to cure a man of smoking by operant conditioning, we should not rely upon the (often impractical) business of associating his smoking with something unpleasant; we should concentrate instead on rewarding him for *not* smoking. As long as our reinforcement of his non-smoking is consistent and thorough, the operant-conditioning theorists hold that this will be a much more effective way of getting him to stop smoking than by treating his smoking as a sign of oral fixation (as the Freudian might), or by giving him any number of lectures on the evils of smoking.

Social-learning theorists accept this operant-conditioning approach, but also lay stress upon providing the subject with models of the reformed behaviour we want from him. Thus, to continue with our example of smoking, the smoker would be exposed to prestigious non-smokers, instead of, as happens more frequently at the moment, to prestigious smokers.

All the above techniques, and particularly those associated with operant conditioning and social learning, are now in wide use, especially in the USA. Since they are used to change all kinds of behaviour, and not just the behaviour of those in need of therapy, the collective title of *behaviour modification* is usually assigned to them (see, for instance, Fontana 1985 for a fuller explanation). Our interest in these techniques lies chiefly in what they can achieve in the classroom, and it is in this context that both Skinner and Bandura have put forward many of their ideas. Perhaps we can best start by taking the example of an isolate child in the infant school, who refuses to mix with the other children. The natural reaction of the sympathetic teacher is to spend much of her time approaching him solicitously and attempting to draw him into group activities. The net result of all this is that often by the end of the term he is no more sociable than he was at the beginning. The teacher may redouble her efforts the following term, but with no better results. What has gone wrong? Well, argue the exponents of behaviour modification, the teacher has actually been *reinforcing* the child's isolate behaviour. She has rewarded him for being an isolate by paying attention to him every time he is on his own. And doubtless, on the occasions when she has succeeded in drawing him into a group, she has then withdrawn her attention from him, thinking it was no longer needed. What she *should* have done is the exact opposite, i.e. to have withheld her attention from the child while he was behaving as an isolate, and to have given it to him every time he made an approach response to other children. In this way, he would have learnt that, instead of getting teacher's attention by being on his own, the way to get it was to be with others.

We can take this model and apply it to other kinds of behaviour. Just as the isolate child was being rewarded for being an isolate, so a child who is not very good at his work may find that the only way he can get his teacher's attention is by playing about. Another child may find that by showing contempt for a subject he can always draw the teacher's attention away from the lesson and into a fruitless attempt to 'convert' him to a better attitude. Another may find that by using bad language he can offend (and therefore strike back at) a teacher he dislikes. Another that he can get more attention from a popular teacher by getting his work wrong than by getting it right. In all cases, the logic of the situation remains the same. The child is being rewarded for the very kinds of behaviour that the teacher wishes to eliminate in him. Defects of personality, Skinner argues, are caused by a misapplication of reinforcers. Study the situation, apply the reinforcers differently, and the defects will be cured (or, more technically, *modified*).

There are several texts available which go into the techniques of behaviour modification exhaustively (e.g. Fontana 1985; Wheldall and Merrett 1984). But basically these techniques can be reduced to a few simple rules.

1   The teacher lists each of the behaviours in a particular child that he wishes to modify. This must be done in detail (e.g. it is not enough just to write down 'rowdiness'; one must break

this down into such things as 'entering class noisily', 'banging desk lid', 'scraping chair on floor'). These are called *target behaviours*.

2   The teacher lists against each of these the target behaviours that are to be aimed for (normally the exact opposite of those in the first list).

3   The teacher analyses precisely how target behaviours in list 1 have been reinforced in the past, and withdraws this reinforcement.

4   The teacher systematically reinforces the target behaviours in list 2.

All this requires skill and patience. It also requires self-control, as when the teacher deliberately ignores a child's noisy entrance into the class, and praises him when he takes his seat quietly. Bandura claims that the teacher can help things along still further by modelling the desired behaviour herself (e.g. by not shouting in class if she doesn't want the children to do so), by drawing favourable attention to children who are modelling the desired behaviour (but only if they are prestigious models), and by always stressing in her instructions to the class the desired rather than the undesired behaviour (e.g. 'Work quietly' rather than 'Stop the noise').

It is also claimed that behaviour-modification techniques can be used to produce less tangible kinds of behaviour such as patience, self-control, determination (in fact the whole range of the things referred to in chapter 5 as traits). This is done by what is called *self-contracting*, a kind of course in self-management. Tharp and Wetzel (1969) report a successful attempt to employ self-contracting in a large secondary school and the surrounding community. Once target behaviours had been listed for individual children, *mediators*, such as parents, local tradespeople and so on, who could provide the children with suitable rewards, were contacted and their help enlisted. Children were then asked to contract to produce desired target behaviours in return for specified rewards. Each time they produced the behaviours (e.g. truthfulness, co-operation, perseverance) they were awarded notations which could be accumulated and then exchanged for the rewards (e.g. extra time watching television, outings, horse rides, helping in a garage, extra pocket money). Within two to six weeks, Tharp and Wetzel claim, 75 per cent of the undesired behaviour had been converted (*turned round*) into desired behaviour. The children had learnt, many of them for the first time in their lives, that things such as honesty may actually pay off. In the course of this learning, they had also acquired a range of other secondary reinforcers as a result of their good behaviour, such as improved school performance, better relationships at home, more teacher approval, more prestige. It is these other secondary reinforcers that prevented the desired behaviour from collapsing once the experiment was over.

Tharp and Wetzel's experiment is really an example, in the normal school setting, of the *token economy* which behaviour modifiers employ in many closed communities such as approved schools, institutions and hospitals, and in which desired behaviour is rewarded with tokens which are exchanged for treats and privileges (see, for instance, Burland 1984). It also indicates to us that rewards must be things that children genuinely desire, and demonstrates that while children are gaining these rewards they are also acquiring more long-term secondary reinforcers, which will sustain their improved behaviour in the future.

Criticism of the learning-theory approach

A whole literature, for and against, has grown up around Skinner's work (see, for instance, Wheeler 1973), and in the short space available here I cannot hope to review it. All I shall try to do is to suggest ways of resolving some of the main areas of disagreement between Skinner and the theorists we have been looking at in previous chapters.

The least controversial part of Skinner's argument, and one that is acceptable to most psychologists, is that we often unwittingly reinforce the very behaviour in children that we wish to discourage. Behaviour-modification techniques provide a very useful way of identifying when this is happening, and of doing something to put it right. It is generally accepted that these techniques work best when they are practised throughout the whole of an institution, which means that if they are tried in a school all the staff should be involved in them, and should work out together a common and consistent programme.

Where Skinner is on more controversial ground is in maintaining that behaviour-modification techniques can correct all
personality problems. His opponents argue that these techniques
tackle the symptoms and not the causes of personality
malfunction, and that, in the long run, new sets of symptoms
are likely to occur in their place. His supporters deny that *symptom
substitution* of this kind does happen, as long as all the relevant
symptoms in a given category of behaviour problems are tackled
in the first place. But, of course, it is often impossible to do this.
In a highly anxious person, for example, particularly one with
free-floating anxiety (see chapter 3), anxiety is a generalised
reaction to pretty well every aspect of his life.

Another point of criticism in Skinner's work is that much
of it (though admittedly by no means all) has been carried
out with animals, and it is doubtful how far the results of this
work can usefully be applied to humans. Because, for example,
we can make an animal behave neurotically, this in no sense
demonstrates that anxiety cannot be caused in man through the
existence of such a thing as a super-ego. The super-ego is a
collection of ideas, values and beliefs acquired and sustained
largely through the use of language. Language gives man a much
wider and more complex range of experiences than have animals,
and allows him to brood on these experiences, to plan future
behaviour, to suffer guilt.

Through the thought processes to which it gives rise, language
also helps man to be *aware of the fact that he is being reinforced*. If
he needs the reinforcement, he produces the appropriate
behaviour to obtain it; if not, he withholds the behaviour.

Skinner, of course, denies that man can choose whether to
produce behaviour or to withhold it, since this would imply that
man has free will, a point that Skinner is not prepared to concede.
Here, inevitably, Skinner is straying into a field beset with all
kinds of philosophical hazards, where 'proof' is not possible one
way or another. Indeed, it is surprising that Skinner, who
describes himself as a scientist, should allow himself to become
involved in a debate of this kind, or to make the kind of
categorical statements concerning it that appear so frequently
in his work.

From our point of view, and surely from the point of view
of any rational person, the important thing is that man thinks

and acts *as if* he has free will. Even Skinner, by exhorting mankind to adopt his operant-conditioning techniques as the only way to make the world safe for future generations (1972), is behaving *as if* man has the freedom to choose whether to accept his advice or not (see Fontana 1984 for a more detailed discussion of these and related issues).

Finally, Skinner's rejection of the notion that man's behaviour can ever be traced to such things as meta needs raises great problems in the explanation of human motivation. It is not easy to see how a simple operant-conditioning model can ever be stretched to explain satisfactorily the work of a Beethoven or a Shakespeare – still less, perhaps, the pleasure that this work has brought to the rest of mankind.

9

Personality and Cognition

Personality and intelligence

To speak of personality *and* intelligence is somewhat misleading, since it suggests that the two are quite separate categories of human psychology. If we accept one of the currently popular operational definitions of intelligence – for instance, that it is the ability to see relationships between things and to use this ability in the solution of problems – we realise that it is very much a part of that general reaction to life that we call personality. When we speak of children as bright, or alert, or dull, it is usually this general reaction that we are talking about, not just the fact that they do well or badly in tests of intelligence. The point is well taken by Cattell, who includes intelligence as one of the factors measured by his personality tests (see chapter 5), and by Kelly (chapter 7).

Perhaps what we should be talking about, therefore, is not whether intelligence interacts with personality but how this interaction operates. Certainly, intelligence seems to influence some areas of personality more strongly than others. Often there does not seem to be any straightforward link between intelligence and a person's beliefs and values (though it will normally affect the manner in which he can defend them). On the other hand, there will be an obvious connection between intelligence and the level of the goals which a person sets himself in life, and between intelligence and the kind of interpretations that he puts upon his life experiences.

Not surprisingly, since intelligence tests are themselves trait-based devices, most of the research into the relationship between intelligence and other factors of personality has been carried out by trait theorists rather than by those who adopt an idiographic approach. With the exception of certain correlations between low intelligence and scores on Eysenck's N dimension (chapter 5), neither Eysenck nor Cattell has found, however, that intelligence correlates *consistently* with any of the dimensions or factors of personality measured in their tests (though we saw, again in chapter 5, some correlation between low intelligence and high L scores).

One very interesting line of research is that carried out by the Fels Institute in the USA into samples of children who, between the ages of six and ten, showed either a marked increase or a marked decline in IQ scores (Kagan et al. 1958). It was found that boys were twice as likely as were girls to be in the group that had shown an increase, while there were more girls than boys in the group that had declined (this may be an indication that boys tend to mature later in measured intelligence than do girls, just as they mature later in speech and in reading skills. Alternatively it may be a cultural thing, with boys receiving more challenge and encouragement once they reach school age than do girls). Children in the increased-IQ group, both boys and girls, were more independent, more competitive, and more verbally aggressive than were those in the declined-IQ group. They were also readier to work hard, showed a stronger desire to master intellectual problems, and were less likely to withdraw in the face of challenge (this compares interestingly with Coopersmith's findings on high self-esteem boys – see chapter 2).

What this research seems to show is that the possession of certain personality characteristics helps children to make full use of their intellectual potential. If we think back to chapter 2, it will be remembered that in higher education Barron produced similar findings in that he found resourcefulness, energy and adaptability correlated well with satisfactory levels of achievement. In one of the most ambitious studies of its kind ever attempted, Terman and Oden (1947) followed up 750 children with IQs of 140-plus into adult life, and found that those who fulfilled their early potential were more interested in their work, more persevering, more self-confident, and better integrated in their life goals. They were also significantly better adjusted and more socially effective than the normal population.

Using the terms which we have used in this book so far, we could say that they were higher in achievement motivation, higher in self-esteem, and better adjusted than the average. All these things, of course, correlate strongly with a secure home background, in which the child enjoys the confidence of his parents, and in which he is set definite and consistent standards and encouraged to reach them. However, as Roe (1953) shows, many eminent scientists have struggled against early feelings of inferiority, and the same is true of many great men, so an unfavourable background by no means *ensures* that a person will make little of his life. Adler (chapter 3) would say that such people are struggling extra hard to compensate for this inferiority. Whether his background be favourable or unfavourable, though, the person who achieves eminence usually seems to be driven by the need to come up to certain expectations, whether they be formed for him by sympathetic but demanding parents, or by the need to prove his worth in the face of indifference or rejection.

More generally, McCandless (1969) suggests research shows that children with high IQs tend to be taller, handsomer, physically stronger and more popular than those at the opposite end of the spectrum. They also tend to be less anxious, partly no doubt because they find life easier to manage than do less able children. In addition they seem better judges of other people (particularly strangers) as well as of themselves, than do less fortunately endowed children. Obviously these high-IQ children will find in the main that people react favourably to them. They will gain a positive opinion of themselves because others have a positive opinion of them. Thus, in the interaction between heredity and environment, the latter will serve to enhance the former, just as the former will help the child more efficiently to come to terms with the latter. Sadly, the less able child will find himself likely to be handicapped by his environment, by people's low expectations of him, by his failure to achieve competence, and eventually by the low opinion of himself that he may develop in the face of the low opinion that others perhaps have of him.

Personality and creativity

This is not the place to enter into a discussion of the nature of creativity. Suffice it to say that psychological research into creativity is of more recent origin than that into intelligence, and that psychologists *suggest* that the latter is characterised by the ability to think *convergently* (i.e. to home in on the unique answer to a problem), and the former by the ability to think *divergently* – that is, to come up with as many solutions as possible to a problem that does not necessarily have a unique answer. Because of the absence of a single right answer, tests to measure creativity are known as *open-ended* tests, and good examples are the 'uses of objects' test (e.g. 'How many uses can you think of for a brick?'), the 'meanings of words' test (e.g. 'How many different meanings can you think of for the word "bolt"?'), and visual tests such as converting as many outline drawings of circles as possible into recognisable objects by simply adding details (see, for instance, Hudson 1966).

It is still not clear whether intelligence tests and divergent-thinking tests are measuring radically different or related human attributes. This is partly because the latter tests are still in a relatively crude, experimental form. However, it does seem clear that a certain level of intelligence is needed if an individual is to be able to organise and use his creative talent effectively, and Canter (1973) suggests that creativity becomes independent of intelligence only at IQ scores of 120 and above. It also seems reasonably clear that there is a relationship between high scores on divergent thinking tests and the possession of certain personality characteristics. In a number of studies using Cattell's 16 PF (see chapter 6), it has been shown that creative people in both the sciences and the arts are more independent, more intellectually self-sufficient, less stable, and more radical than the average (see, for instance, Cattell and Butcher 1968). Scientists tend to score highly on withdrawal behaviour items, while artists (particularly painters) score on unconventionality and eccentricity (the 'artistic temperament' perhaps). Taylor and Holland (1964) add to this list by suggesting that evidence shows creative people are more autonomous, self-sufficient, self-assertive, and resourceful, while attention has already been drawn (see chapter 6) to the link between creativity and scores on

Eysenck's P dimension. They are also more introverted, more inclined towards feminine interests, more aware of their impulses, and more open to the irrational in themselves. Barron (1979), in a study of 1500 creative men and women in a wide range of fields, found them to reveal in their life histories all kinds of outlandish behaviour, including depression, tension, anxiety, psychosomatic illness, suicide attempts and various criminal offences. At the risk of lengthening this list too far, we can add that other investigators have found creative people to have a high tolerance of ambiguity (they enjoy puzzling over things that have many possible solutions), and to be capable of a high level of abstract thought. As with intelligence, most studies indicate that people who make effective use of their high levels of creativity are generally strong on achievement motivation. They have a single-mindedness which enables them to work hard in their chosen field and to show a high level of interest and involvement in the things that they do (compare the comments on the mature personality in chapter 2).

As with intelligence, however, it must be stressed that creativity should not be seen as something distinct and separate from personality. The creative person is creative in his whole approach to life. Many of the personality characteristics that we mentioned above are not just things that the creative person happens to have: they *are* his creativity as it reveals itself in the business of everyday living. When it comes, therefore, to discussing how best the teacher can encourage creativity in children, much of what has already been said in this book about the teacher's role in helping the child towards maturity and self-actualisation of personality will still apply. Rogers stresses that positive regard and empathic understanding are, as with other areas of personality, the most important contribution the teacher can make towards fostering creativity in children, and to these he adds a *freedom from external evaluation*. This means that, although the teacher is free to *react* to children's creative work (i.e. to say whether she likes it or not), she should refrain from passing categorical judgements upon it (i.e. saying it is 'wrong' or 'bad'), since by its very nature divergent activity contains no immutable rules of correctness.

The important part that the teacher can play in allowing the child sufficient freedom to develop his creative powers (Jung would say, in freeing the child to listen to his own unconscious – see chapter 3) is evidenced by a number of studies (e.g. Haddon and Lytton 1968) which show that children in informal primary schools perform better on divergent-thinking tests than do children in formal schools, and that this enhanced performance persists when the children transfer to secondary schools, irrespective of the type of secondary school involved (Haddon and Lytton 1971). What this really means is that, if the teacher wishes to encourage the creative side of a child's personality, the child must not be taught to reject this side of himself, and to adopt only a conventional approach to thinking. Hudson (1966) found a tendency amongst boys specialising in science subjects at sixth-form level to think convergently, while those specialising in the arts tended to think divergently, and this could well be evidence that some teachers of science subjects are not prepared to allow as much self-expression in their pupils as are some teachers of arts subjects (mistakenly, we might add, as there is just as much need to think creatively about science as there is about the arts). It seems that, when children who are highly convergent are encouraged to be freer and less judge-mental in their responses, their ability to think divergently increases markedly.

Jerome Bruner and his colleagues, in a number of studies (e.g. 1956), speak of *holistic* (creative) thinking and *algorithmic* (rational) thinking, and consider that our Western educational system encourages the latter at the expense of the former. We lay stress upon conformity, upon children always arriving at the same conclusions as the teacher, upon children always using the 'right' method for solving problems in mathematics and science, upon children not guessing solutions (frequently *guessing*, Bruner argues, is evidence of creative effort, or a sudden flash of insight), upon children not tolerating ambiguity. It is not that Bruner, or indeed any psychologist, argues against the need for convergent, algorithmic thinking, but simply that this kind of thinking should not be the only form of thought encouraged in children. McKellar (1957) puts the case well when he talks of holistic (or, as he chooses to call it, 'autistic') thinking as being the *author* of any worthwhile creative act, while rational thinking is the *editor* who sifts through the ideas generated by holistic thinking, isolates those which are most relevant, and puts them to use (see also Fontana 1985b).

There is evidence that teachers sometimes find it harder to relate to children high on creativity than to other children. Getzels and Jackson (1962) certainly found this to be the case in their, admittedly rather narrow, sample of teachers and children. They suggest that the creative child's non-conformity and apparent self-sufficiency can make him less immediately sympathetic to teachers than are children with more conformist attributes.

If Getzels and Jackson are right, this means that teachers may sometimes have to take particular care not to allow the creative child's independent outlook to count against him. But this probably applies to all gifted children, whether their giftedness lies in very high creativity, very high intelligence, or both. It is probably another of the failings of the British educational system that it pays insufficient attention to helping the gifted child to live with, and to make good use of, his gifts. Sometimes, though probably not as often as writers in the British press have taken to claiming, the highly gifted child can feel as isolated from other children as can the child of correspondingly low ability. He can also feel as misunderstood and unappreciated. With his high level of curiosity and activity, and his boredom in the face of unchallenging work, he can be a generally uncomfortable member of the class, and some teachers, not surprisingly, feel threatened by his precocious knowledge, and are convinced that he is setting out to score off them in front of the class.

Perhaps because of their very feeling of separateness, there is some evidence that gifted children (particularly, it seems, gifted girls) play down their gifts to avoid antagonising the teacher, and to avoid unpopularity with the rest of the class. Such self-rejection may be potentially as damaging to the personality as are the other forms of self-rejection that we looked at in chapters 3 and 4. The cost to the nation in terms of lost potential needs no emphasising.

Cognitive style

Cognitive-style theorists start from the accepted fact that we are bombarded by so many data from the environment every moment of our lives that we cannot possibly attend to them all without enormous cognitive strain. They then ask *how* do we sort these data out and decide what to attend to and what not, and suggest that we do it by *coding* them – that is, by placing each of them into one of a range of categories which carries its own rating of importance. In any situation, things belonging to categories relatively high in importance gain our attention; those belonging to categories relatively low do not.

The way in which we assign things to categories will be partly determined by previous experience, and partly by innate factors, including how we actually *perceive* things (e.g. some people are innately more sensitive to certain stimuli, such as loud noises, bright colours, subtle differences in shape, than are others). We can get a good example of coding from a child tackling a problem. First he studies and categorises the information it contains. Next he hunts through the information in his head until he finds data coded into a similar category. Finally, he forms an hypothesis and sees if it will solve the problem.

Cognitive-style theorists claim that we carry out this coding-process in our own characteristic and consistent way. We do not change our method drastically from problem to problem. Since our whole contact with the outside world, including our social behaviour, is influenced by the way in which we code, it must be seen as a part, and an important part, of our personalities.

Cognitive-style theory is not, however, an alternative to the other theories of personality that we have been looking at. It does not concern itself with motivation, or with the possible systems within the personality, such as the ego and the super-ego, which help to determine why people differ in the degrees of importance which they attach to various categories. For the most part, it seems content to accept that neurotic people may put things into categories which have to do with their worries, and then attend to those which they find the most threatening. It accepts that the extrovert may tend to code in terms of his prefer-ences as an extrovert, and the introvert in terms of his preferences as an introvert. It accepts that coded categories may become built into personal constructs and so on. It is not so much a theory of personality as an attempt to explain the actual mechanisms that the personality uses to interact with the world. It is concerned with the way in which we think, and not with why we think in this way or with the content of our thoughts.

We can illustrate this by going back to our example of a child tackling a problem at school. One child may characteristically read quickly through the problem, get an overall, and perhaps inaccurate, picture of what it is all about, and immediately start trying to solve it. Another might characteristically read it through slowly, word by word, before starting work. These different methods of tackling the problem are part and parcel of the children's respective cognitive styles. However, such things as the level of enthusiasm which they bring to bear upon the task, the degrees of importance which they assign to the respective categories which it contains, and the amount of anxiety which they feel if they get it wrong, belong not to their cognitive styles but to those areas of their personality and of their learning discussed in earlier chapters.

Obviously, from an educational point of view, cognitive style is an important aspect of personality. We often find ourselves saying that one child tends to rush things, that another always seems to miss the essentials in an argument, that another is disorganised in his thinking, that another is precise and methodical, and so on. The characteristics represented by these labels are evidenced not only in the way in which children solve problems, but also in the way in which they relate to other people, and in such things as the amount and depth of consideration which they give to their selection of short-term and long-term life goals.

However, terms such as 'disorganised', 'inconsistent', 'methodical' are somewhat vague and subjective, and various attempts have been made by psychologists to see if there are any more precise – albeit broad – categories of cognitive style into which people can be divided. The results of this research have proved to be rather similar to those produced by the trait-based approach to personality theory detailed in chapter 6, in that they have tended to identify bipolar dimensions. These dimensions are still very much in the experimental stage, and the tests upon which they depend are still crude. It is not clear, either, to what extent or in what way they relate to each other, or to personality theories. Nevertheless, three of them are of sufficient interest to be looked at closely: namely, *field dependence–independence*, *focusing–scanning* and *reflectivity–impulsivity*.

Field dependence–independence   In one way it is a little unfair to talk of the dimension of field dependence–independence as being still in the experimental stage, since it has been the subject of a formidable amount of research over the last fifteen years, chiefly by Herman Witkin and his colleagues. The impetus for Witkin's work came from the discovery by the United States Air Force that many pilots, on losing visual contact with the ground (as, for example, when they flew into a dense cloud bank), lost all sense of the vertical, and, if unaided by instruments, would often end up unwittingly flying upside down (with consequent increase in combat vulnerability!).

Witkin attempted to study this phenomenon experimentally by constructing the Body Adjustment Test, in which subjects were seated in a tilting chair facing into a small box-like 'room' which could also be tilted (Witkin 1959). When taking the test, some subjects proved able to say whether they were upright or not irrespective of the angle of the chair and of the 'room', while others lost their sense of the vertical completely as soon as the 'room' in front of them started to tilt; some of them even claimed to be upright when the room and chair were both tilting through an angle of thirty degrees. What seemed to be happening was that the first group of subjects were able to sort out the pull of gravity (the relevant stimulus) from the visual experience of the 'room' in front of them (the irrelevant stimulus), whilst the second group were not. Witkin terms the first group field-independent (FI) and the second group field-dependent (FD).

Further experiments, using both the embedded-figures test, in which the subject first studies a simple black-and-white line pattern and then has to pick it out when it is 'hidden' in a more complex pattern, and the rod-and-frame test, in which the subject sits in a darkened room and attempts to place in the vertical a luminous rod which is surrounded by a tilted luminous frame, confirmed the existence of field dependence and field independence as two extremes of a dimension, with the majority of the population, as in the dimensions discussed in chapter 6, located somewhere in the middle.

Witkin then established that this dimension has interesting applications in everyday life. For example, FD people seem less able to pick out and remember the details in a given situation that can FI people. When presented with a battery of projective techniques (see chapter 3), they also disclose themselves as less perceptive in dealing with life, and more easily influenced (Witkin et al. 1954). Witkin sums this up by saying that the FD person has a *global* cognitive style, while the FI has an *articulated* one (these terms, 'global' and 'articulated', together with the group label *psychological differentiation*, are sometimes used as alternatives to 'field dependence–independence').

Since correlations have been found between extroversion and field dependence (Witkin 1959), it is tempting to suggest that the latter is to some extent an expression of the former. The extrovert, with his greater social involvement, his greater need for frequent and varied stimuli, and his slower rate of conditioning, pays less attention to each unit of experience, is more readily swayed by group opinion, and gives himself less time to be perceptive about which are the most relevant units of experience in any given situation. He is therefore logically somewhat more likely to be FD than is the introvert.

However, it would be wrong to regard the dimension of field dependence–independence as lying precisely along the same dimension as extroversion–introversion. Though there is a correlation, it is far from being a perfect one. Many extroverts are FI, just as many introverts are FD. For field independence also seems to go with certain things that extroverts possess as frequently as do introverts, such as a more developed sense of personal identity (which in Erikson's terms, remember, indicates maturity of personality – see chapter 2), and with higher self-esteem and self-confidence. Interestingly, it also goes with a particular style of ego-defence mechanism (see chapter 3). Bertini (1961) demonstrates that when FI people employ repression, they seem able to repress selectively, whereas FD people are likely to repress indiscriminately, blotting out large chunks of their past experience in a way which suggests they are much less able, consciously or unconsciously, to single out the precise causes of their anxiety. FD people are also better able than are FI people to keep their feelings separate from their thoughts and perceptions, which could be one of the reasons why field dependence is more apparent in women than in men.

It is important to stress that, although much of what we have been saying seems to favour field independence over dependence, Witkin is at pains to point out that, as with something such as extroversion–introversion, neither is invariably 'better' than the other. The FD person might be more sensitive to the needs of others than is the FI, more gregarious, more socially involved, perhaps less likely to withdraw. *Extremes* at either end of the dimensions are equally adverse, with the FD person tending to suffer from identity defusion and overdependence upon others (alcoholics and compulsive overeaters are often FD), and the FI person from a too-rigid defence of personal identity which leads him to lay the blame for his problems always upon others rather than to blame (and try to change) himself.

Field dependence–independence has obvious implications for the teacher in terms of children's interpersonal relationships and their approach to problem-solving. Although it throws little light on creativity (different kinds of creativity may possibly demand different kinds of style), it does have bearings upon intelligence. Studies show that FI children perform better on analytical items in IQ tests than do FD, though there is no difference on verbal items. Witkin (1965) argues that, as many educationally subnormal (ESN) children also score more highly on analytical items than they do on verbal, and that as many children with low analytical scores are often not diagnosed as ESN because this poor performance is disguised by high verbal ability, IQ tests should be replaced by those for cognitive style, since the latter are more comprehensive and 'recognise the rooting of intellectual functioning in personality'.

Focusing–scanning is associated particularly with Jerome Bruner. Unlike Witkin, Bruner has obtained the main impetus to his work from research with children. Again unlike Witkin, he has concentrated his research upon observing the coding-systems (called by Bruner *strategies*) which are adopted in a problem-solving situation. One of Bruner's best-known tests is to present the child with a number of pairs of cards, one pair at a time, each card consisting of varying arrangements of squares, circles, lines and colours. The child is then told that one card in each pair is 'correct' and the other 'incorrect', and, as more of the pairs are presented to him, he is asked to determine what particular features of the squares, circles, or whatever, denote 'correctness' or 'incorrectness' (Bruner et al. 1956).

Research of this kind appears to indicate that children are distributed along a dimension at one end of which are those who examine the relevant features in each of the pairs until they have amassed enough information to advance an hypothesis (the *focusers*), and at the other end are those who form an hypothesis on the basis of the first pair, stick to it until eventually enough subsequent pairs have been examined to show it to be untenable, and then have to go back to the beginning and start again (the *scanners*).

What seems to be happening is that focusers characteristically delay hypothesis-making until they have enough evidence, while scanners characteristically form an hypothesis on slimmer evidence, and have no option but to begin afresh if subsequently they are shown to be wrong. If the same strategies are applied in social situations, we might say that the focuser makes up his mind about other people only when he has got to know them well, whereas the scanner makes up his mind more quickly, sometimes only to have to abandon this opinion altogether (and along with it, perhaps, a friendship), when the evidence against it becomes too strong.

The importance to teachers of the focusing–scanning dimension is considerable. Children who scan, it seems, have a particular need to be allowed to go back and check earlier clues if their original hypothesis becomes untenable, and therefore may be at a disadvantage in mentally presented problems. Children who focus, on the other hand, may delay too long over forming their hypotheses, and thus be handicapped in work involving quick responses. On the teacher's own part, there is the risk that the scanner may make snap decisions on children, and then have to recant later (e.g. with such remarks in a school report as 'Has deteriorated this term, must do better next', which may confuse the child as much as it worries his parents), while the focuser may be overcautious in giving praise, or good marks, or in writing an enthusiastic report or reference.

Ideally, people should be able to focus or to scan, depending upon the nature of the problem they are called upon to tackle, the amount of time in which they have to do it, and so on. Sometimes a quick hypothesis is called for, sometimes a more cautious one. Extreme focusing can be a sign of insecurity (if you never reach a decision about anything, you can never be proved wrong) and may lead to sitting on the fence until the opportunity has been lost (e.g. someone else proposes to the girl). Extreme scanning on the other hand can mean an early commitment with little hope of retrieving the situation later (the wedding-bells sound too early). When solving each problem, one should be a good judge of how long one can delay one's decision while awaiting further evidence.

Again, there are no clear correlations between focusing–scanning and creativity (or between it and intelligence). Probably extremes of either are less helpful than a judicious combination of the two. There is also little link between Bruner's dimension and Witkin's (scanners are not, as one might suppose, FD, and focusers FI), though it is not unreasonable to hope that future research, with more sophisticated measuring devices, may reveal a relationship of some kind between them.

Reflectivity–impulsivity The third dimension that we are to examine is proposed by Jerome Kagan. If we think back to the beginning of this section, it will be remembered that there are typically three stages in problem-solving: first, categorising the given information; second, sifting mentally through one's own knowledge to find similar categories; and, third, forming an hypothesis with which to proceed to the solution. Kagan considers that cognitive style particularly influences the first and last of these stages. Some people, he claims (1966), characteristically act *reflectively* in categorising the information and producing their hypotheses, whilst others behave *impulsively*.

Kagan also claims to have discovered another dimension, *visual analysis*, which relates to the extent to which people break down the information in stage one. Some people, at least with a visually presented problem, tend to break it down into small units, whilst others prefer to work with much larger chunks of it. Perhaps oddly, there is no strong correlation between visual analysis and reflectivity–impulsivity. Some reflective people work with large chunks of information and some with small, and the same is true of impulsive people.

Kagan has devised a number of tests to explore these two dimensions. In the Delayed Recall of Design Test, which is a test of reflectivity–impulsivity, the child is presented with a simple black-and-white design for a few seconds, and is then asked to pick it out from a number of similar designs. The test is scored for response time and for accuracy, and, typically, reflective children take longer over their responses and make fewer errors than do impulsive children. In the Visual Analysis Test, the child learns to associate, respectively, four nonsense syllables with four complex designs, each containing several components, and is then asked to produce the correct syllable when he is shown only single components abstracted from each design. The visually analytic child, who has had no difficulty in analysing each design into its separate components, makes far fewer mistakes than does the unanalytic child, to whom each of the designs exists only as a complete unit.

Like Witkin's and Bruner's, Kagan's work has important potential implications for education. At present, most of these implications must be drawn from the reflectivity–impulsivity dimension, as the visual analysis dimension is still very much in the experimental stage. Leaving aside a small group of highly anxious children who have a long response time and still make many errors, it seems clear that, on challenging and difficult problems at least, reflective children make significantly fewer errors than do impulsive ones. Kagan (1966) claims that they show a strong desire to be right first time, and seem able to tolerate the ambiguity of a long silence (not easy if perhaps both teacher and class are waiting impatiently to see if they know the answer or not) while they weigh each possibility before responding. Impulsive children, on the other hand, adopt a 'shotgun' approach, firing out several answers, either in the hope that one will prove correct or because they rely upon feedback from the teacher rather than upon their own internal reflections to tell them if they are getting 'warm' or not. Kagan says that reflective children have a slow, and impulsive children a fast, *conceptual tempo*.

Conceptual tempo also seems important in serial learning-tasks. For example, when learning vocabulary lists, impulsive children tend to make more errors of commission (i.e. including extra words in the recalled list) than do reflective children, and, the more critical the teacher becomes, the more of these errors they make. When reading, they tend to make more orthographic errors, typically by misreading simple three-letter words (e.g. 'log' for 'dog', 'cat' for 'pat'), even when they are perfectly familiar with the individual letters concerned.

Like Witkin and Bruner, Kagan resists the conclusion that it is necessarily 'better' to be reflective than impulsive, though the former does seem associated with maturity in that as children grow older their reflectivity scores tend to increase (though the *relative* differences between impulsive and reflective children may remain the same). He suggests that, whereas high reflectivity may be advantageous in academic subjects such as mathematics, it may be a disadvantage in the visual arts and in some aspects of the humanities and social sciences. However, Kagan does concede that the highly impulsive child's frequent experience of selecting the wrong hypothesis may be a source of discouragement, and lead to increased anxiety and greater impulsivity as he tries to put things right.

Further research into cognitive style

It is by no means clear whether it is possible to change a child's cognitive style on any of the dimensions mentioned. Relative positions on each of them seem to remain markedly stable over the years, and Kagan concludes that cognitive style may be a 'basic component of the individual's behavioural organisation' (1966). More research is needed before the point is proved, and it is to be hoped that such research will also show whether tests of cognitive style are the improvement on tests of intelligence that Witkin claims them to be, and whether they can be usefully used by teachers when deciding how best to structure the learning-situation to suit individual children.

We also need to know more about the relationship (if any) between the various dimensions of cognitive style so far discovered. Kagan (1976) suggests all these dimensions can be grouped into three main types. Type I consists of those dimensions which compare the subject's performance against a predetermined standard of correctness (as for example in field dependence–independence, where the subject is required to solve problems such as the embedded-figures test). Type II consists of those dimensions where there are no 'right' or 'wrong' answers, but where the psychologist makes a value judgement (as for example in focusing–scanning, where in some situations the former might be rated more appropriate, in others the latter). Type III includes those dimensions where neither performance standards nor value judgements are involved (as, for example, in a style known as *cognitive width*, which simply seeks to establish variations between peoples' respective views on such things as the range of circumstances in which specified events are likely to occur). Other investigators, however, identify as many as nineteen separate types, and the whole subject must therefore still be seen as very confused (see, for instance, Goldstein and Blackman 1978 for a survey).

Finally, we need to know more about the relationship between cognitive styles and intelligence and creativity, respectively, and much more about the relationship between cognitive styles and the causal factors in personality development. As we have seen, a start has been made in relating cognitive style to ego-defence mechanisms, to personal identity, and to particular forms of personality problems. But what part does an individual's sense of security, of confidence, of self-esteem, etc. have to play in his style? And is style more a product of, or cause of, these things? And how does cognitive style affect the way in which one forms one's personal constructs, or the freedom with which one moves through one's life space, or the methods which one employs to deal with cognitive dissonance? The subject is rich in research possibilities.

10

Teacher Personality

Various references have been made throughout the book to teacher personality, and the time has now come to draw these together and amplify them. Clearly, just as children's personalities influence what happens in the classroom, so do the personalities of teachers. To complicate matters, teacher and child personalities also interact with each other, sometimes beneficially and at other times less so. For example, in chapter 6 attention was drawn to the fact that on occasions introverted teachers may work best with introverted children, and extroverted teachers with those who are extroverted, and in chapter 7 it was stressed that teachers should be able to induce telic or paratelic states in themselves and in their class as the need arises. Teachers who remain out of harmony with their children in personality terms, making demands upon them for behaviours that children find difficult to produce, are unlikely to provide the kind of environment in which learning can most effectively take place.

It seems best, however, to open this chapter by looking at teacher personality in general terms. Beginning with trait theories, is there any evidence that across the whole range of teaching-activities there is one particular kind of personality likely to meet with the greatest success?

Trait theories and teacher personality

The answer is, very little, perhaps because of the very complexities to which I have just drawn attention. In spite of a great deal of time and research effort devoted to the search for correlations between scores on trait inventories and teaching-success, results have proved for the most part disappointing. The three tests most widely used in this research, the MMPI, the 16PF and the Eysenck Personality Inventory, have produced confusing findings, with qualities such as Cattell's 'parmia' and 'surgency' proving important in some studies and not in others, with extroversion sometimes correlating with teaching-success and sometimes not, and even with significant levels of neuroticism and mental instability (on the MMPI) often failing to predict a lack of success. One of the most ambitious of all research initiatives into teacher personality, that of Ryans in the USA in 1960, actually went to the lengths of constructing a special scale, the Teacher Characteristics Rating Scale, but failed to produce anything beyond the finding that successful teachers are slightly more understanding, warm, friendly, responsible, systematic, stimulating, imaginative and enthusiastic than their less successful brothers and sisters. But even these low correlations held only for the primary school.

Another approach which at one time looked promising was to measure teachers' attitudes towards education, in the belief that successful teachers would show up as much more positive and committed. A scale widely used in Britain for this purpose is that of Oliver and Butcher (1968) which groups teacher attitudes into three categories labelled respectively *naturalism*, *radicalism* and *tender-mindedness*, but to date research has turned up little of value beyond the fact that student teachers tend to increase their scores on all three variables during training only to slip back again once they get into the profession. This accords with the findings of a longitudinal study by Cortis (e.g. 1973 and 1985), who also found that successful teachers tend to be rather conventional and non-progressive in their attitudes. However, he has established that they are able to put the school's interests before their own, whereas unsuccessful teachers, though apparently more progressive, are inclined to put their own interests before those of the school and to be dominant, suspicious and aggressive.

Research has revealed a rather more clear-cut picture in higher education, and particularly within universities. Murray (1980) presents an extensive review of the literature, but a representative picture emerges from recent findings by Rushton and his colleagues (e.g. Rushton and Murray 1985). Using student ratings of lecturer effectiveness, Rushton demonstrates that two composite dimensions which he calls *achievement orientation* (composed of traits such as dominance, ambition, leadership, intelligence and endurance) and *interpersonal orientation* (composed of traits such as supportiveness, non-authoritarianism, non-defensiveness and objectivity) appear together to account for the main personality characteristics associated with successful teaching. To these, again on the strength of student ratings, can be added two classroom behaviour dimensions, namely *charisma* (made up of qualities like expressiveness and interest in subject) and *organization* (clear and well-organized lecture material). High scores on these four factors, plus successful interaction between each of them, seem to be what mark off the good lecturer in student eyes from the mediocre.

We cannot be sure that these findings would hold good at school level, or even with less able adult students, though if they were more broadly interpreted and more oriented towards the individual needs of children it is reasonable to assume that they might do so. But research of this nature is easier at higher education than at school level, since we can invite students to do the ratings of teacher effectiveness, and the function of the university lecturer is less complex and more readily defined than is that of the class teacher. Indeed the problem of defining and thus of identifying the successful teacher is the main obstacle to research of this kind in schools. It is a problem that is likely to tax politicians and administrators even more in the future, with the trend towards increasing in-service assessment of teacher competence. For teaching is a multi-skilled profession, and it is doubtful if outsiders, whether they be Her Majesty's Inspectors or even head teachers, can be relied upon to make effective distinctions between the abilities of all but the very good and very bad practitioners.

It is interesting to see how research has failed to back up what could be termed the 'common sense' picture of the successful teacher. If asked, most people would probably guess that the good teacher is usually extroverted and outgoing, with a high level of stability. Not only does research provide little support for this view, but the teaching-profession as a whole comes out as no more extroverted or stable than the general population (Eysenck 1964). Whatever qualities of personality the good teacher needs, it seems clear that they do not show up readily on trait measures.

State theories and teacher personality

It will be clear from chapter 7 that the state approach to personality looks at teacher personality from a very different angle. Bloom (1983) argues that we must jettison the idea of seeking for fixed personality characteristics in teachers, and instead think in terms of affective task entry behaviours, just as we should with children. Before entering upon a particular lesson or upon a particular encounter with children (whether it be a learning-encounter, counselling, or even out-of-school activity) the teacher should determine what particular affective behaviours on his part are likely to obtain the best results. This sounds rather like trying to be all things to all men (or to all children), but Bloom would argue that we are not asking the teacher to change her basic personality, even if a state theorist believes in the existence of such a thing, but simply asking the teacher to exercise her range of professional skills. At times in school she needs to be a leader and to take the initiative. At other times she needs to know when to keep silent and be a good listener. At times she needs to be decisive and authoritative, at other times to leave things more flexible or to encourage democratic processes. At times she needs to provide children with clear answers to their questions; at others she needs to be more enigmatic, and to prompt the children into finding the answers for themselves. With some children she needs to be challenging and stimulating, with others supportive and encouraging. With some children she can be trusting; with others she needs to be a little more careful. And so the list goes on. She must even recognise those occasions when she can readily share a joke with the class, and those occasions when she has to be wary lest certain members of it overstep the mark.

All these qualities are, let us repeat, professional skills rather than fixed personality characteristics. Some of them are readily cultivated; others take a little more time. But no competent teacher will find them beyond her scope. Indeed, in some instances it is simply a matter of allowing existing personality states to become more open and apparent. The teacher may, for example, be enthusiastic about teaching and about her specialist subject, but fail to show this enthusiasm when with children. Or she may be very sympathetic towards children's personal problems, but fail to indicate that she is always ready to discuss these problems individually when the need arises. Or she may be inclined towards patience with slow learners, but feel she has to hide this inclination in the mistaken belief that all children respond best to challenge. In all these instances, what is required is simply enhanced understanding of children and an enhanced readiness to communicate this understanding, rather than far-reaching changes in teacher personality.

Teacher moods

An important factor in the state-based approach to personality is, as indicated in chapter 7, the question of moods. We discussed in chapter 7 the problem of children's moods, but teachers have moods too (as do we all). And, just as children's moods can disconcert the teacher, so the teacher's moods can disconcert her children. The best practical advice that can be offered here is that the teacher should try at all times to be aware of her changing moods and of the effect they have upon her behaviour. Since children thrive best on consistent treatment (see chapter 2), a teacher whose moods swing wildly from day to day is hardly likely to get the best out of them. Children come to respect teachers with whom they know where they stand, and the teacher who carefully observes her own emotional states lessens the risk of inflicting on one class a rather angry mood induced by the earlier behaviour of another. Similarly, she can lessen the risk of carrying into school a bad mood prompted by something that happened that morning at home. The ability to master one's moods usually comes only with long practice, but by studying our moods closely we can at least stop ourselves from taking them out unfairly upon others.

On the question of moods, Apter's work (1982) indicates the extent to which many people fluctuate during the day. As part of his research, people were assessed at regular intervals during working hours over a period of time, and it was noted not only how rapidly in a majority of instances their moods changed but also how closely related these mood changes were to external events such as an interview with the boss or a quarrel with a colleague. Such changes in mood coloured attitudes towards events and towards people in a significant way. That is, the manner in which we experience the world, interpret the motives of others, reach decisions, and the like, depends in part at least upon the mood we are in at the time concerned.

Apter's work has not yet been replicated with teachers, but it is fair to assume that they are often subject to the same rapid mood changes, particularly as they face a wider range of stimuli and pressures than do people in most other walks of life. The lesson to be learnt is that, when we observe our moods and discover them to be changing rapidly (or even slowly) as a consequence of events or of other people's behaviour, we should ponder why we are so much at the mercy of externals. I may very well claim that '4B make me so angry' or that 'Peter makes me impatient' or that 'Marion depresses me', but is this really accurate? I am not a robot which has on its forehead buttons labelled 'anger' or 'impatience' or 'depression' which 4B or Peter or Marion can come up and press. In the end, however difficult it may be to appreciate initially, we create our own moods. Certainly these moods may be reactions to 4B or to Peter or to Marion, but in the final analysis they are our creation and not theirs. We must ask ourselves whether we are really prepared to have our moods dictated to us by the actions of the children we teach, and, if we are not, then we must take steps to change ourselves.

This is not easy, but the first step has already been indicated: namely, to observe ourselves more closely to see what moods we are experiencing and what external events seem to be associated with them. The next step, where these events cannot be changed in any way, is to see what it is in ourselves that triggers off our emotional reactions to them. What is it in me that prompts anger at the behaviour of 4B, or impatience at the behaviour of Peter, or depression at that of Marion? Is it my sense of professional pride that is being wounded, or an unrealistic desire to get children to learn more quickly than they are able, or a wish to have the world a very much different place from what it actually is? Whatever factors in me are prompting my reactions, once I have identified them I can begin to work on them. 4B make me angry because I see them as a direct threat to my sense of personal and professional worth, but in fact 4B behave badly with most members of staff. Their behaviour is not a threat to me as a person, but a consequence of their general boredom with school. The best I can hope to achieve with them therefore is to arouse *some* signs of interest, *some* signs of co-operation, *some* signs of progress.

Similarly with Peter. He is not a slow learner on purpose as a way of exhausting my patience. He is a slow learner because to date school work has not been presented to him in a way that he can understand. The answer lies in trying new methods with him, in getting him to work more at his own pace, in giving him the experience of success that will build up his self-esteem and interest and confidence in both himself and in what goes on in school. Similarly with Marion. Her morose behaviour is not designed to depress me. It is simply an indication of her unhappy life and of her problems in making friends and of getting on with her family. It is in the nature of things for children to have problems, and it is part of the task of the school to recognise these problems and to help with their solution.

Of course it may be said that there are occasions when 4B really *do* want to make me angry, and when Peter wants to make me impatient and Marion does want to make me depressed. If this is the case, then by reacting as I do then the children are succeeding in their intentions. My reactions will even potentially reinforce their behaviour (see chapter 8), since they may enjoy seeing me angry/impatient/depressed. I now have to ask myself whether I want children to have this kind of success. If I do not, then the answer once more is to look at my emotional life and ask myself again what it is in me that prompts my emotional reaction.

We are not going to achieve overnight success, but by working on our emotions in this way we shall gradually begin to see more clearly what is going on in our emotional life, and through this clarity begin to find ways of bringing this life more under our own direction. Not only will this make us more effective teachers (and human beings): it will also cut down on the incidence of teacher stress, which brings us to our next section.

Teacher stress

Teaching is a stressful profession in view of the manifold demands made upon the teacher and the often inadequate conditions in which she has to meet them. Owing to its link with the emotions, stress is an area of personality study, and much has been written on its deleterious effect upon both the individual's psychological and physical well-being.

In personality terms, the stress-prone teacher is less the nervous individual or the one low in self-confidence than the individual who is overdedicated to work and takes things too seriously (Kyriacou 1982). Whether we blame others for our professional problems or blame ourselves (external or internal loci of control – see chapter 5), overdedication and overseriousness seem to be in the end the two key factors. This is not because these things in themselves necessarily lead to stress, but because they are frequently associated with a hard-driving, determined state of mind which becomes impatient with opposition and frustrated at failures (a syndrome of behaviour which has been referred to in the medical literature as the 'Type A' personality, and which seems to be significantly implicated in the onset of coronary heart disease). This state of mind can lead the individual to push himself too hard, constantly at war within himself and with others over the issues which impede what he sees as desirable progress. Inevitably, in any walk of life, such as teaching, where the constraints and obstacles are many and where the indicators and rewards of success are often less than clear-cut, individuals locked into this state of mind are likely to suffer accordingly.

This may seem like advising the teacher not to bother very much about her work if she is to remain stress-proof, but this is not so. The advice is simply that the teacher should be realistic about what can be achieved and what cannot, given the constraints under which she has to work, and that she should be able to laugh a little when things go wrong.

A sense of humour is not only of great value in itself, since the act of laughing helps to reduce tension, but because, as discussed in chapter 2, it appears to be linked to self-insight. It is an indication that we can chuckle over ourselves and even over the people and things we love without harming our love for them. It indicates that we have a sense of proportion, even over those issues which are most precious to us in life. A sense of humour shows that we have the insight to recognise that for all of us there is often a gap between pretension and performance. We set out with high intentions, yet find ourselves making a complete mess of things. But it is also the ability to realise that the only proper response to this is not an orgy of breast-beating and vilification, but amusement, leaving us with the courage and energy to try again. Falling short of our goals is no good or useful reason for thinking the less of ourselves or of others. It is simply the way life *is*. Similarly, through this self-insight we have to accept that we cannot be equally successful at all aspects of life, whether it be personal life or professional life. We may admire the way a colleague gives up hours after school every night, and drive ourselves to do even better. We may admire the scholarship of another colleague, the success with remedial classes of another, the sporting-prowess of a third, the organising and administrative ability of a fourth, the amazing memory for children's names of a fifth, but we cannot hope always to emulate them. We simply have to do the best we can, knowing that inevitably we shall often fall short of what we hope for or of what others seem able to achieve (just as they may feel secretly that they fall short of us in certain respects), and accept once more that this is simply the way life *is*. Certainly we should try and develop our skills and improve our performance, but we can only do this within a context that is sensible and realistic. And, in the end, nobody is going to benefit if we drive ourselves into ill health.

Although nervousness and low self-confidence are not linked to stress in the way that an overdemanding and overserious personality is, they nevertheless cause teachers considerable problems which are best dealt with in this section. Trait-based theories see anxiety as a relatively fixed characteristic (see chapter 6), dependent largely upon innate factors. State-based and humanistic theories (and to a certain extent social and field theories) do not deny that inborn temperament may make some of us more prone to feel the tremors of anxiety more readily than others, and that this in turn feeds back into our cognitive states and makes us more fearful of facing those events that cause this anxiety. But they nevertheless place far more emphasis upon anxiety as a transient experience. Even the most anxious amongst us is unlikely to be anxious *all* the time. So the task becomes to identify what makes us anxious, and how we experience and cope with this anxiety (see chapter 7).

Psychologists generally agree that anxiety is a response to threat. We feel something or somebody is threatening some aspect of ourselves or of the people or things important to us. In dealing with this anxiety (or fear, if we prefer to call it such), the first step, as with other emotions, is to observe ourselves closely to see when fear arises and what kind of things appear to prompt it in ourselves. The next step, again as with other emotions, is to ask what is it in us that feels threatened and why. Are we being physically threatened? Not usually. Is it the small child in us, that part of our psychological life that still reacts with habitual fear when those in authority are at odds with us as it did in childhood? Quite possibly. Is it a fear of being thought inadequate or incompetent by others? Again, quite possibly. Is it a fear of thinking *ourselves* inadequate? Equally possibly. And so on. When identified, most of these things can be seen to be largely illusory, things that can in time be remedied. Childhood fears are no longer relevant to the daily experiences of adult life. Others may not be thinking us inadequate, and – if they do – well then, so be it. That is their prerogative. In both personal and professional affairs we cannot allow our emotional life to be governed simply by the opinions of others. And, as to thinking ourselves inadequate, this is often linked to problems of self-esteem (see chapter 2), problems which can be countered by taking a more realistic and encouraging view of ourselves, learning indeed to accept ourselves as we are, instead of standing like an eternal critic at our own elbow and finding fault with everything we do.

Physical relaxation techniques, and simple meditation practices in which we train the mind to concentrate calmly and peacefully upon the breathing (see Fontana 1985a) are also a great help to the teacher in coming to realise that the mind need not be allowed constantly to brood over fears and problems and over the emotional reactions that go with them, but instead can be turned at will to focus upon those things that we choose for ourselves. In meditation it becomes possible even to introduce into our thoughts those things that usually cause a stab of panic (4B on a Monday morning, for example) and to contemplate them in our peaceful state without any emotional reaction at all. Practice of this kind makes it increasingly easy to face hitherto frightening events in daily life, and to see that our one-time fear reaction is not inevitable at all, but is a product of habit and of inappropriate use of our own minds. The equanimity with which we can contemplate events during meditation gradually begins to carry over into real life and into these events themselves.

Space does not allow us to discuss relaxation and meditation techniques in detail, and in any event these things are best learnt from a teacher. But, for those who want a specialist reference, Leshan (1983) is a good place to start. The overall point being made in this chapter is that teachers, just like children, should be subject to growth and development. Schools are educational institutions, and the education should not only be for the pupils. Owing to the teacher's professional interest in developmental processes, owing to the richness of the opportunities for self-awareness that are given to us when we work with children, and owing to the very real need to find ways of countering professional stress, the teacher should be as closely involved in her own psychological growth as she is in that of her class. And, of course, by and through her own development throughout her professional life, the teacher becomes increasingly able to offer the consistent understanding, warmth and guidance upon which children best flourish.

11

Extreme Personality Problems

In the discussion of Freud's contribution to psychology (in chapter 3), it was stated that he has given us the notion that normal and abnormal behaviour are simply different points on the same continuum. To some degree we all have personality problems, and decisions on when these problems become bad enough to be classified as causing extra behaviour problems or as giving rise to neuroses or psychoses are largely cultural ones. Such decisions differ from society to society, from generation to generation, and from individual to individual.

Much of what we can say about personality problems has already been said in earlier chapters, and the purpose of the present chapter is more to discuss definitions than to go back over ground already covered. This is particularly true of maladjustment, which we shall look at first.

Maladjustment or extreme behaviour problems

I have deliberately avoided these terms throughout the book, but, in a sense, I have been talking about them every time I have made any mention of the problems that can occur in the developing personality. Such terms are often taken to mean the behaviour of particularly unruly, violent and disruptive children, which is why I have steered clear of them, but in fact they mean all children who are experiencing special problems in relating to others and to themselves. The Underwood Report (1955) defined the maladjusted child as 'one who is developing in ways that have a bad effect on himself or his fellows, and cannot without help be remedied by his parents, teachers, and other adults in normal contact with him'.

Though this definition begs such questions as 'What is meant by "a bad effect"?' it is a useful one in that it obviously includes within the scope of maladjustment the withdrawn and iso- lated child as well as the gang-leader, the nervous and highly- strung child as well as the violent one, the child who cannot communicate as well as the one who communicates too loudly and selfishly.

In the course of the book enough has been said about these problems to show that to a marked degree their causes lie in faulty relationships between the child and his parents or substitute parents, particularly during the first five or six years of his life, but essentially throughout the whole of his childhood and adolescence. Low self-esteem, high levels of guilt, reinforcement incorrectly applied, constant demands for inappropriate behaviour, the absence of love and of emotional security, the absence of sympathy and understanding – all these things help make the maladjusted child. Psychologists may disagree about the actual mechanisms involved, but they all accept that maladjustment is usually indicative of a child who is largely the victim of the inadequacies of his elders. The child who is forced to live with inconsistency or with fear and with a sense of rejection, the child who is forced to live with conflict between the various areas of his life or who is constantly reminded of his own inadequacies, is hardly likely to learn to relate to the world around him in a positive and satisfying way.

Enough has been said, too, about these problems to show that their treatment lies largely in reversing the processes that have caused them. Acceptance in the place of rejection, concern in the place of uninterest, sympathy in the place of indifference, consistency in the place of inconsistency, encouragement in the place of censure, harmony in the place of conflict. But there remains one point that we still have to stress. The class teacher, with her class of thirty children and all the numerous demands that are made of her, cannot hope to set the world to rights on her own. Even if she did have more time to spend with the individual victims of maladjustment, she shares only a part of a child's life. The child belongs to the world outside school as well as to the world inside. He belongs to the home and the peer group, to the values of his local community, and, although the teacher may be able to do a great deal to help him, she cannot be expected to do it all.

This is why, to return to the Underwood Report's definition of maladjustment, the problem of the maladjusted child 'cannot be remedied by his parents, teachers, and other adults in normal contact with him'. The maladjusted child, in other words, needs specialist help. So part of the teacher's job with such children is therefore a diagnostic one. She should be able to identify anyone in her class who may be maladjusted, and then refer him, through the head teacher, for assessment and possibly for treatment by the child-guidance service. Having done so, she must try to see that the referral is carried out.

Hyperactivity

Hyperactivity is a personality disorder that is often dealt with under maladjustment, but it merits a separate section since it is not clear that it really stems from the same causes. Hyperactivity, as the name suggests, is constant and extreme restlessness. The term is used to cover a range of restless and uncontrolled behaviours, though Barkley (1983) considers that inattention, impulsivity and non-compliance are the most important of them. Not surprisingly, hyperactive children's school work has been found to be well below average.

Hyperactive behaviour seems to manifest itself as early as the first year of life, and to persist through into adolescence. At one time a commonly accepted theory was that it is owing to brain damage, but research has found no evidence for this. Nor is there any obvious causal factor in the environment, as there typically is in maladjustment (though some maladjusted children do exhibit hyperactivity amongst their other symptoms). The cause, it seems, may be some chromosomal abnormality, and it is known that the condition can sometimes be medically controlled with amphetamines, which act indirectly upon the hypothalamus (one of the areas of the brain that, as we saw in chapter 5, may be involved in some way in personality). Marston and Scott (1970), who call the condition 'Inconsequentiality' (or 'Q'), and suggest it is related to high impulsivity scores on Kagan's reflectivity–impulsivity dimension (see chapter 9), also consider it may be congenital in origin, because hyperactive children are generally poor scorers on such tests of innate ability as motor performance.

The hyperactive child can be a great strain on the teacher's patience. In addition to the main characteristics identified by Barkley and mentioned above, he has also found hyperactive children to suffer from poor peer relations, to be immature and generally below average in intelligence, to be easily frustrated, low in self-esteem, and to tend towards short physical stature and a range of physical allergies. Something like 4 per cent of children may fall into this category, with boys outnumbering girls by six to one. The teacher should remember that the hyperactive child may have little conscious control over his behaviour. There is no point in insisting that he keep still, and it may be that it is the very frustrations and checkings that he receives from adults which lead to his insolence and clowning, and to his low self-esteem. It may even be that it is these that sometimes cause the maladjustment in those instances where maladjustment and hyperactivity go together.

Ideally, the hyperactive child should be given scope by the teacher for his constant need for activity. A long attention span should not be demanded of him, and of course he should never be labelled as meddlesome, or as a nuisance; nor should he be made to feel odd in any way. As such children are usually extroverted, they should never be denied group work whatever problems this may bring, and they sometimes, in fact, respond well to the opportunities of group leadership. There is some evidence that behaviour-modification techniques (see chapter 8), which involve praising them for periods of concentration and co-operation, and for the initiative and inventiveness which they often show, are of value in helping them learn self-control (see Fontana 1985a).

Psychopathy (or sociopathy)

Psychopathy is an extreme form of personality disorder, often correlated with delinquent and anti-social activity. Fundamentally, the psychopath is a person who cannot experience the emotions normally present in interpersonal behaviour. He seems unable to feel affection, sympathy or remorse. He is selfish, superficial, and indifferent both to the feelings of others and to fear or punishment. He demands instant gratification for his own impulses, regardless of the long-term consequences to himself or to other people. He has a pathological disregard for the truth, and can be distinguished from other neurotic or emotionally disturbed children by his complete absence of guilt.

Psychoanalysts would argue that the psychopath is someone who has failed to develop a super-ego, and someone in whom even the ego seems insufficiently reality-oriented. The reasons for this failure seem to be both physiological and environmental. Summarising research into the former, Hare (1970) suggests that psychopathy may be related to brain immaturity, as even in adult life psychopaths show an excessive amount of the slow brain-waves usually found in children. Of more relevance in the light of our discussion of the physiology of extroversion–introversion and neuroticism–stability (see chapter 6), the psychopath seems to have a low level of arousal in the autonomic nervous system. Perhaps he therefore needs an excessive amount of stimulation to achieve the 'kicks' that arousal of this system brings. Eysenck, whose P dimension measures some of the factors associated with psychopathy, suggests that the condition may be linked to a degree of unstable extroversion so extreme that it is way beyond the range measured by the dimension.

Environmentally, psychopaths often come from broken and loveless homes, with fathers who are alcoholic or themselves psychopathic. There is some suggestion that the psychopath may be modelling the cold and inconsistent behaviour of his parents, while Arieti (1967) thinks he may be a victim of a complete lack of impulse-training and of social control. However, in view of the early age at which psychopathy typically manifests itself, it is probable that genetic factors outweigh environmental ones in importance.

No reliable evidence exists on the incidence of psychopathy in the population, though it is known that males far outnumber females. Distressingly, there is often little that the teacher can do to help the psychopath. The latter's callous and sadistic behaviour, and his constant betrayal of trust, may outrage the teacher, but, since the psychopath seems unable to experience remorse, moral lectures and appeals to his better nature usually have little effect. Psychopaths are generally of normal intelligence, and can learn things unconnected with emotional responses readily enough, which often means they quickly find out how to manipulate others. Thus, instead of their usual callous aggressiveness, they may adopt with those who are trying to help them a guise of charming plausibility, or may become parasitic, relying upon apparent helplessness and repeated, insincere promises of remorse and of atonement to get their own way.

Like the teacher, the psychologist has no markedly effective means of rehabilitating the psychopath. Sometimes the latter seems to settle into more reasonable social behaviour in adult life, but in many cases effective treatment, if it comes, may rely upon psycopharmacology (mood-changing drugs), or upon long-stay institutional care, probably with the consistent application of behaviour-modification techniques.

Neurosis and psychosis

There is sometimes confusion in people's minds between mental illness (psychosis) and the extreme forms of the anxiety that we have been referring to throughout the book (neurosis). This is not surprising, as the distinction is by no means a clear one. However, it is generally accepted by psychologists and by psychiatrists that, whereas *neurosis* allows the subject to carry on the semblance of a normal life, often with the awareness that he is seriously disturbed and needs help, in *psychosis* he is unable to do so and requires hospitalisation. Typically, the psychotic patient is unaware that he is ill, and seems to have lost contact with reality. Unlike neurotic behaviour, it is possible that psychotic behaviour is not on a continuum with normal behaviour (Maher 1970), though, as we shall see shortly, it is possible that it owes its origin to some of the same causes.

We have already discussed neurosis in earlier chapters, and there is no need for further detailed amplification at this point. Suffice it to say that the term 'neurosis' covers extreme and persistent anxiety states, in which the individual may be well aware that he is worrying over unnecessary trivia or over imagined disasters but is relatively powerless to halt the process. Often this anxiety is linked with depression, with feelings of pointlessness and of personal inadequacy, and with depleted physical energy and zest for living. The possible causes and treatment of neurosis (or *neuroses*, if we prefer to use the plural term) are fully covered in chapters 2 to 5.

Turning to the psychoses, it is important to stress that these fall within the province of clinical rather than educational psychology. It would therefore be inappropriate to spend too much time on them, but generally they are categorised into two distinct, though perhaps overlapping, forms, *schizophrenic* and *manic–depressive*. A third form, *paranoic*, is possibly a subdivision of the former. In schizophrenic psychosis (schizophrenia), which accounts for the largest single group of patients in our mental hospitals, the individual sometimes loses all sense of personal identity. He suffers from auditory and visual hallucinations, he may show deviant motor behaviour (e.g. retaining the same position for long periods), perceptual abnormalities (colours and sounds may become intense, or he may lose his sense of his own body image) and, most strikingly of all, he may show thought disorders which rob him of the ability to communicate logically with others. In the course of these disorders, he may withdraw altogether from human contact, or he may show an incompatibility between the idea which he is trying to express and the emotion that accompanies it – hence the term 'split personality' which is sometimes applied to schizophrenics (e.g. he may talk of sad things with joy and of joyful things with sadness).

In manic–depressive psychosis, the patient often retains some measure of rapport with others, but his behaviour is characterised by violent mood swings, from extreme elation (mania) to extreme despondency (depression). Sometimes these swings are brought about by environmental factors, but more often they are spontaneous, and any attempt to reason with the patient usually meets with failure. In paranoia, the patient may remain more coherent than the schizophrenic, but he shows the same capacity for delusions, except that these are consistently organised into two kinds: delusions of his own importance, and delusions that others are persecuting him.

Little is certain about the causes of mental illness. There is some evidence to link schizophrenia with introversion, and manic–depressive psychosis with extroversion (Eysenck 1969), and this suggests there may be a constitutional factor of some kind at work here (a suggestion supported by Sheldon's findings that schizophrenia is more common amongst ectomorphic people and manic–depressive psychosis amongst endomorphs – see chapter 1). However, the old idea that mental illness is directly inherited is untenable, though people may differ in their resistance to the pressures that bring on this illness.

Extensive but inconclusive research has been carried out into the nature of these pressures, particularly with schizophrenia (see Lowe 1969 for a survey). The consensus seems to be that these pressures begin in early childhood, and are of the same order as those implicated in the neuroses, except that in schizophrenia there may often be present what Bateson and his colleagues (1956) call the *double-bind* situation. This situation is a form of inconsistency, particularly within the mother–child relationship, in which the child habitually has certain kinds of behaviour demanded of him and then is criticised for producing them (as, for example, when the mother tells the child not to pester her with his chatter, and then accuses him of sulking when he tries to be quiet). The double bind punishes the child emotionally whatever he does, and he has no chance to acquire the capacity to distinguish logic in human behaviour. Not surprisingly, he withdraws increasingly from relationships with others. Bannister (1960) suggests that in terms of construct theory (see chapter 7), the double bind means that the child's personal constructs are constantly being invalidated. Laing and Esterson (1964) present several case studies illustrating the double bind in action, and also some of the other emotional pressures that the schizophrenic person can come under from his family, in particular from a mother who is often dominating and restrictive, and who consistently interprets her child's behaviour in terms of the effect that this behaviour has upon her own feelings and upon her personal well-being, health, outlook on life, and so on.

The causes of manic–depressive psychosis have attracted less attention. Psychoanalysts hold manic depression to be a sign that, through psychological frustrations in the very early years of life, the individual is still fixated in the infantile feeding-cycle of hunger ('depression') and satiety ('mania'). Other studies suggest it is linked with a sense of repressed failure, which on occasion overwhelms the individual and from which he attempts to break free.

Perhaps it is a sign of our confusing times that mental illness is on the increase. At some time in our lives, more than one in ten of us will need psychiatric help, women being more vulnerable than men. Ryle (1969) shows that the problem is not an inconsiderable one amongst students in higher education, and schizophrenia, in particular, sometimes manifests its presence as early as the adolescent years. The treatment of mental illness belongs to the consulting-room and not to the school, but the teacher should be alert for the symptoms, and prompt to refer the child concerned for specialist help.

Briefly, in schizophrenia these early symptoms often involve increasingly withdrawn behaviour, in which the adolescent or young adult seems unable to relate satisfactorily to others, and may even show sudden and apparently groundless suspicion and hostility towards them. There may be a marked deterioration in his standards of personal appearance, and in his study habits and his general ability to organise his life. Subsequently, these symptoms may become further complicated by irrational and even bizarre thought patterns, and an inability to follow a consecutive or logical argument, or to manifest the kind of emotions that others feel are appropriate.

In manic–depressive psychosis, the symptoms may take a rather different, less irrational form, with the individual showing extreme restlessness or uncharacteristic apathy or, disconcertingly, violent and unaccountable fluctuations between the two. Initially, study habits and thought patterns are less likely to suffer than in schizophrenia, and, far from withdrawing, the individual may show increased demands upon the company and support of others. But, as with schizophrenia, the need for specialist help becomes increasingly apparent, and, the sooner this help is given, the more promising the long-term prognosis.

The reader wishing to know more about this important area is referred to Morris and Kratochwill (1983), who discuss fully the diagnosis, incidence and treatment of neuroses and psychoses in children.

Conclusion

I have ended this book with a chapter on personality problems, and psychologists are commonly accused of looking too frequently on the negative side of human personality rather than on the positive. This is partly, of course, because so much of their work has been with people who have problems. Like the medical doctor, the psychologist often tends not to see much of people when they are well. Many of our insights into personality come, therefore, from the clinical work of people such as Freud, Rogers or Kelly, and even personality tests for general use often have their origin in tests designed for use with the mentally ill.

But, this being said, I hope I have stressed strongly enough that few psychologists now see the normal and the abnormal personality as two quite separate things. Whether it be Freud talking about normal and abnormal behaviour as being on a continuum, or Eysenck measuring neuroticism by a single dimension somewhere on which we all find our place, psychologists stress that through the study of even the most unfortunate and disturbed of our fellow men we gain insights into what it means, essentially, to be human.

Perhaps we can leave this point by saying that humanistic psychologists in particular, but probably all psychologists in their heart of hearts, see man as characterised by joy as well as by suffering, by hope as well as by despair. The teacher is uniquely placed to see both sides of man, and to see them, moreover, as they develop from the experimental world of childhood to the more formed and self-assured one of late adolescence and early adulthood.

The other thing I hope I have stressed enough is that, although psychologists' ideas about personality seem to cover such a disparate range, there is a pattern there, if we look for it – not always a harmonious pattern, and not always a very finished one, but a pattern nevertheless. Although psychoanalysts may argue with behaviourists, and behaviourists with humanists, the teacher, who is a practical person and has to get on with the business of educating children, can learn something from them all. The trouble with conflict, in any academic discipline, is that it sometimes tends to polarise opinion unnecessarily. People take up opposing positions, and ignore the common ground that exists between them. Psychologists, at times, make too much of their differences, and not enough of their similarities.

Finally, I hope the book makes it clear that each child, each individual personality, is unique. Children share the same needs, and the same kind of developmental pattern, but the emphasis for each child is different. That is why teaching can be such a difficult task. There are no glib formulas that work for everybody, in every case. Which means, as many of the psychologists we have been discussing would insist, that to relate to children we must learn to understand their individual psychological worlds and their individual constructs. Only then can we really help them become confident, open and hopeful adults.

References

Adler, A. (1939) *Social Interest*. New York: Putnam.

Allport, G. W. (1961) *Pattern and Growth in Personality*. London: Holt, Rinehart and Winston.

Andry, R. (1960) *Delinquency and Parental Pathology*. London: Methuen.

Antony, W. S. (1973) 'The development of extroversion, of ability, and of the relation between them', *British Journal of Educational Psychology* 43, 3.

Apter, M. J. (1982) *The Experience of Motivation*. London: Academic Press.

Arieti, S. (1967) *The Intrapsychic Self*. New York: Basic Books.

Asch, S. E. (1955) 'Opinions and social pressure', *Scientific American*, November.

Bandura, A. (1969) *Principles of Behavior Modification*. New York: Holt, Rinehart and Winston.

Bandura, A. (1973) *Aggression: a social learning analysis*. Englewood Cliffs: Prentice-Hall.

Bannister, D. (1960) 'Conceptual structure in thought disordered schizophrenics', *Journal of Mental Science* 106.

Barker Lunn, J. C. (1969) 'The development of scales to measure junior school children's attitudes', *British Journal of Educational Psychology* 39, 1.

Barkley, R. A. (1983) 'Hyperactivity'. In R. J. Morris and T. R. Kratochwill, *The Practice of Child Therapy*. New York and Oxford: Pergamon Press.

Barron, F. (1954) 'Personal soundness in university graduate students', *Publications in Personality Assessment and Research no. 1*. Berkeley: University of California Press.

Barron, F. (1979) *The Shaping of Personality*. New York: Harper and Row.

Bateson, G., Jackson, D., Haley, J., and Weakland, J. (1956) 'Towards a theory of schizophrenia', *Behavioral Science* 1.

Bennett, S. M. (1973) 'A re-evaluation of the JEPI', *British Journal of Educational Psychology* 43, 2.

Bertini, M. (1961) 'Il tratto dell'isolamento nella sua determinazione dinamica e strutturale', *Contributi dell'Instituto di Psicologica* 25.

Bigge, M. L. (1982) *Learning Theories for Teachers*, 4th edn. New York: Harper and Row.

Bloom, B. S. (1983) *Human Characteristics and School Learning*. New York: McGraw Hill.

Brown, J. A. C. (1964) *Freud and the Post Freudians*. Harmondsworth: Pelican.

Bruner, J., Goodnow, J., and Austin, G. (1956) *A Study of Thinking*. New York: Wiley.

Burland, R. (1984) 'Behaviourism in the closed community: the token economy and performance contracting'. In D. Fontana (ed.), *Behaviourism and Learning Theory in Education*. Edinburgh and London: Scottish Academic Press.

Callard, M. and Goodfellow, C. (1962) 'Neuroticism and extroversion in schoolboys as measured by the junior MPI', *Journal of Educational Psychology* 61.

Canter, S. (1973) 'Some aspects of cognitive function in twins'. In G. S. Claridge, P. Canter and W. I. Hume (eds), *Personality Differences and Biological Variations: a study of twins*. Oxford: Pergamon.

Cattell, R. B. (1980) *Personality and Learning Theory*. New York: Springer.

Cattell, R. B. and Butcher, H. J. (1968) *The Prediction of Achievement and Creativity*. New York: Bobbs-Merrill.

Cattell, R. B. and Kline, P. (1977) *The Scientific Analysis of Personality and Motivation*. London: Academic Press.

Caudill, W. and Weinstein, H. (1966) 'Maternal care and infant behaviour in Japanese and American middle class families'. In R. Konig and R. Hill (eds), *Yearbook of the International Sociological Association*.

Chanan, G. and Delamont, S. (eds) (1975) *Frontiers of Classroom Research*. Slough: NFER.

Child, D. (1970) *The Essentials of Factor Analysis*. London: Holt, Rinehart and Winston.

Church, J. (1976) *Understanding Your Child From Birth to Three*. London: Fontana.

Clarke, A. M. and Clarke, A. D. B. (eds) (1976) *Early Experience: myth and evidence*. London: Open Books.

Conger, J. J. and Miller, W. C. (1966) *Personality, Social Class, and Delinquency*. New York: Wiley.

Coopersmith, S. (1968) 'Studies in self-esteem', *Scientific American*, February.

Cortis, G. A. (1973) 'The assessment of a group of teachers in relation to earlier career experience', *Educational Review* 25, 2.

Cortis, G. A. (1985) 'Eighteen years on: how far can you go?' *Educational Review* 37, 1.

Crutchfield, R. S. (1955) 'Conformity and character', *American Psychologist* 10.

Davie, R., Butler, N., and Goldstein, H. (1972) *From Birth to Seven*. London: Longman.

Elliott, C. D. (1972) 'Personality factors and scholastic attainment', *British Journal of Educational Psychology* 42, 1.

Entwistle, N. J. (1968) 'Academic motivation and school attainment', *British Journal of Educational Psychology* 38, 2.

Entwistle, N. J. (1972) 'Personality and academic attainment', *British Journal of Educational Psychology* 42, 2.

Entwistle, N. J., Nisbet, J., Entwistle, D., and Cowell, M. (1971) 'The academic performance of students', *British Journal of Educational Psychology* 41, 3.

Erikson, E. H. (1950) *Childhood and Society*. New York: Norton.

Erikson, E. H. (1959) 'Growth and crisis in the healthy personality'. *Psychological Issues* 1.

Erikson, E. H. (1971) *Identity: youth and crisis*. London: Faber.

Eysenck, H. J. (1956) 'The inheritance of extroversion–introversion', *Acta Psychologia* 12.

Eysenck, H. J. (1978) *You and Neurosis*. London: Fontana.

Eysenck, H. J. (1983) 'Human learning and individual differences', *Educational Psychology* 3, 3–4.

Eysenck, H. J. (1985) *The Rise and Fall of the Freudian Empire*. Harmondsworth: Penguin.

Eysenck, H. J., Arnold, W. J., and Meili, R. (1975) *Encyclopedia of Psychology*, vol. 2. London: Fontana/Collins.

Eysenck, H. J. and Cookson, D. (1969) 'Personality in primary school children'. *British Journal of Educational Psychology* 39, 2.

Eysenck, H. J. and Eysenck, S. G. B. (1964) *Manual of the Eysenck Personality Inventory*. London: University of London Press.

Eysenck, H. J. and Eysenck, S. G. B. (1969) *Personality Structure and Measurement*. London: Routledge and Kegan Paul.

Eysenck, H. J. and Eysenck, S. G. B. (1976) *Psychoticism as a Dimension of Personality*. London: Hodder and Stoughton.

Eysenck, S. G. B., Nias, D., and Eysenck, H. J. (1971) 'The interpretation of children's lie scale scores', *British Journal of Educational Psychology* 41, 1.

Eysenck, H. J. and Wilson, G. (1973) *The Experimental Study of Freudian Theories*. London: Methuen.

Festinger, L. (1962) 'Cognitive dissonance', *Scientific American*, October.

Fonagy, P. (1981) 'Research on psychoanalytic concepts'. In F. Fransella (ed.), *Personality: theory, measurement and research*. London: Methuen.

Fontana, D. (1983) 'Individual differences in personality: state based versus trait based approaches', *Educational Psychology* 3, 3-4.

Fontana, D. (ed.) (1984) *Behaviourism and Learning Theory in Education*. Edinburgh and London: Scottish Academic Press.

Fontana, D. (1985a) *Classroom control: understanding and guiding classroom behaviour*. London: British Psychological Society/Methuen.

Fontana, D. (1985b) 'Creativity in the educational context'. In M. J. Apter, D. Fontana, and S. Murgatroyd, (eds), *Reversal Theory: current trends and developments*. Cardiff: University College Cardiff Press.

Freud, S. (1953-64) *The Complete Psychological Works*, 24 vols, ed. J. Strachey. London: Hogarth Press.

Furneaux, W. D. (1957) 'The use of psychological tests for the selection of students to the department of aeronautics', Imperial College Report (unpublished).

Getzels, J. W. and Jackson, P. W. (1962) *Creativity and Intelligence*. New York: Wiley.

Glueck, S. and Glueck, E. (1956) *Physique and Delinquency*. New York: Harper and Row.

Goldfarb, W. (1955) 'Emotional and intellectual consequences of psychologic deprivation in infancy; a re-evaluation', in P. Hoch and J. Zubin, (eds), *Psychopathology of Childhood*. New York: Grune.

Goldstein, K. M. and Blackman, S. (1978) *Cognitive Style: five approaches and relevant research*. New York: Wiley.

Gray, J. A. (1985) 'A whole and its parts: behaviour, the brain, cognition and emotion', *Bulletin of the British Psychological Society* 38, April.

Haddon, F. H. and Lytton, H. (1968) 'Teaching approach and the development of divergent thinking abilities in primary school children', *British Journal of Educational Psychology* 38, 2.

Haddon, F. H. and Lytton, H. (1971) 'Primary education and divergent thinking abilities - four years on', *British Journal of Educational Psychology* 41, 2.

Hall, C. and Lindzey, G. (1970) *Theories of Personality*. New York: Wiley.

Hare, R. D. (1970) *Psychopathy: theory and research*. New York: Wiley.

Hargreaves, D. (1967) *Social Relations in a Secondary School*. London: Routledge and Kegan Paul.

Harlow, H. F. and Harlow, M. H. (1962) 'Social deprivation in monkeys', *Scientific American*, November.

Harlow, H. F. and Harlow, M. H. (1966) 'Learning to love', *American Scientist* 54, 3.

Hartshorne, H. and May, M. (1928) *Studies in the Nature of Character*. New York: Macmillan.

Hess, E. H. (1970) 'The ethological approach to socialization', in R. Hoppe, G. Milton and E. Simmel (eds) *Early Experiences and the Processes of Socialization*. New York: Academic Press.

Hinkle, D. (1965) 'The Change of Personal Constructs from the Viewpoint of a Theory of Implications' (unpublished PhD thesis, Ohio State University).

Hudson, L. (1966) *Contrary Imaginations*. Harmondsworth: Pelican.

Jakubczak, F. and Walters, R. (1959) 'Suggestibility as dependency behaviour', *Journal of Abnormal Social Psychology* 59.

Jung, C. G. (1953–) *Collected Works*. Princeton: Princeton University Press.

Kagan, J. (1966) 'Developmental studies in reflection and analysis', in A. Kidd and J. Rivoire (eds) *Perceptual Development in Children*. London: University of London Press.

Kagan, J., Sontag, L., Baker, C., and Nelson, U. (1958) 'Personality and IQ change', *Journal of Abstract Social Psychology* 56.

Kelly, G. (1955) *The Psychology of Personal Constructs*, 2 vols. New York: Norton.

Kelvin, P. (1970) *The Bases of Social Behaviour*. London: Holt, Rinehart and Winston.

Kelvin, P., Lucas, C., and Ojha, A. (1965) 'The relation between personality, mental health, and educational performance in university students', *British Journal of Social Clinical Psychology* 4.

Kline, P. (1983) *Personality: measurement and theory*. London: Hutchinson.

Koch, H. (1956) 'Sissiness and tomboyishness in relation to sibling characteristics', *Journal of General Psychology* 88.

Kogan, N. (1976) *Cognitive Styles in Infancy and Early Childhood*. Hillsdale, NJ: Lawrence Erlbaum.

Lacey, C. (1970) *Hightown Grammar*. Manchester: Manchester University Press.

Laing, R. D. and Esterson, A. (1964) *Sanity, Madness and the Family*. London: Tavistock.

Lam, Y. L. J. (1982) 'Selected course content, cognitive and affective factors and classroom behaviours of adult learners', *British Journal of Educational Psychology*, 52, 3.

Leith, G. and Trown, E. A. (1970) 'The influence of personality and task conditions on learning and transfer', *Progress in Learning and Educational Techniques* 7.

Le Shan, L. (1983) *How to Meditate*. Wellingborough, Northants: Turnstone Press.

Lewin, K. (1935) *A Dynamic Theory of Personality*. New York: McGraw-Hill.

Lewin, K. (1942) 'The relative effectiveness of a lecture method and a method of group decision for changing food habits', Committee on Food Habits, National Research Council.

Lewin, K., Lippitt, R., and White, R. (1939) 'Patterns of aggressive behavior in experimentally created "social climates" ', *Journal of Social Psychology* 10.

Lewis, M. (1972) 'State as an infant-environment interaction: an analysis of mother–infant behavior as a function of sex', *Merrill-Palmer Quarterly in Behavioral Development* 18.

Lowe, G. R. (1969) *Personal Relationships in Psychological Disorders*. Harmondsworth: Penguin.

Lynn, R. (1971) *An Introduction to the Study of Personality*. London: Macmillan.

Maher, B. A. (1970) *Principles of Psychopathology*. New York: McGraw-Hill.

Marston, N. and Scott, D. (1970) 'Inconsequence as a primary type of behaviour disturbance in children', *British Journal of Educational Psychology* 40, 1.

Maslow, A. H. (1970) *Motivation and Personality*. New York: Harper and Row.

McCandless, B. (1969) *Children: behaviour and development*. London: Holt, Rinehart and Winston.

McDonald, L. (1968) *Social Class and Delinquency*. London: Faber.

McKellar, P. (1957) *Imagination and Thinking*. London: Cohen and West.

McLelland, D. C. (1961) *The Achieving Society*. Princeton: Van Nostrand.

Mead, M. (1935) *Sex and Temperament in Three Primitive Societies*. New York: Morrow.

Mehrabian, A. (1969) 'Measures of achieving tendency', *Educational Psychological Measurement* 29.

Milgram, S. (1974) *Obedience to Authority: an experimental overview*. London: Tavistock.

Morris, R. J. and Kratochwill, T. R. (1983) *The Practice of Child Therapy*. New York and Oxford: Pergamon.

Murray, H. G. (1980) Evaluating University Teaching: Toronto, Ontario: Confederation of University Faculty Associations.

Mussen, P. H., Conger, J., and Kagan, J. (1984) *Child Development and Personality*. New York: Harper and Row. 6th edition.

Newman, H., Freeman, F., and Holzinger, K. (1937) *Twins: a study of heredity and environment*. Chicago: University of Chicago Press.

Oliver, R. A. and Butcher, H. J. (1968) 'Teachers' attitudes to education', *British Journal of Educational Psychology* 38, 1.

Osgood, C. E., Suci, G., and Tannenbaum, P. (1957) *The Measurement of Meaning.* Urbana: University of Illinois Press.

Parnell, R. W. (1958) *Behaviour and Physique.* London: Edward Arnold.

Price, W. and Whatmore, P. (1967) 'Behaviour disorders and pattern of crime among XYY males identified at a maximum security hospital', *British Medical Journal* 1.

Ravenette, A. (1975) 'Grid techniques for children', *Journal of Child Psychology and Psychiatry* 16.

Riding, R. J. (1977) *School Learning: mechanisms and processes.* London: Open Books.

Robertson, J. (1962) 'Mothering as an influence in early development', *Psychoanalytical Studies of the Child* 17.

Roe, A. (1953) ' A psychological study of eminent psychologists and anthropologists, and a comparison with biological and physical scientists', *Psychological Monograms* 67, 2.

Rogers, C. R. (1957) 'The necessary and sufficient conditions of therapeutic personality change', *Journal of Consulting Psychology* 21.

Rogers, C. R. (1961) *On Becoming a Person.* Boston, Mass.: Houghton Mifflin.

Rogers, C. R. (1974) 'In retrospect: forty-six years', *American Psychologist* 29.

Rosen, B. C. and d'Andrade, R. G. (1959) 'The psychosocial origin of achievement motivation', *Sociometry* 22.

Rosenberg, M. (1965) *Society and the Adolescent Self-Image.* Princeton: Princeton University Press.

Rosenthal, R. and Jacobson, L. (1968) *Pygmalion in the Classroom.* New York: Holt, Rinehart and Winston.

Rotter, J. B. (1966) 'Generalised expectancies for internal versus external control of reinforcement', *Psychological Monographs* 80.

Rushton, J. (1966) 'The relationship between personality characteristics and scholastic success in eleven-year-old children', *British Journal of Educational Psychology* 36, 2.

Rushton, J. P. and Murray, H. G. (1985) 'On the assessment of teaching effectiveness in British universities', *Bulletin of the British Psychological Society* 38, November.

Ryans, D. G. (1960) *Characteristics of Teachers.* Washington DC: American Council on Education.

Ryle, A. (1969) *Student Casualties.* Harmondsworth: Allen Lane.

Satir, V. (1972) *Peoplemaking.* Palo Alto, California: Science and Behavior Books.

Scheinfeld, A. (1973) *Twins and Supertwins.* Harmondsworth: Penguin.

Sears, R., Maccoby, E., and Levin, H. (1957) *Patterns of Child Rearing*. Evanston, Ill.: Row Peterson.

Semeonoff, B. (1976) *Projective Techniques*. New York: Wiley.

Semeonoff, B. (1981) *Projective techniques*. In F. Fransella (ed), *Personality: theory measurement and research*, London: Methuen.

Sheldon, W. H. (1954) *Atlas of Men*. New York: Harper and Row.

Sheldon, W. H., Lewis, N., and Tenney, A. (1969) 'Psychotic patterns and physical constitution'. In D. Sankar (ed.), *Schizophrenia, Current Concepts and Research*, New York: PJD Publications.

Shields, J. (1962) *Monozygotic Twins*. London: Oxford University Press.

Skinner, B. F. (1972) *Beyond Freedom and Dignity*. London: Jonathan Cape.

Skinner, B. F. (1974) *About Behaviourism*. New York: Knopf.

Smith, P. B. (1981). 'Research into humanistic personality theories'. In F. Fransella (ed.), *Personality: theory measurement and research*. London: Methuen.

Smith, P. K. (1974) 'Ethological methods'. In B. Foss (ed.) *New Perspectives in Child Development*, Harmondsworth: Penguin.

Taylor, C. and Holland, J. (1964) 'Predictors of creative performance'. In C. Taylor (ed.), *Creativity, Progress and Potential*, New York: McGraw-Hill.

Terman, L. and Oden, M. (1947) *Genetic Studies of Genius IV*. Stanford: California University Press.

Teyler. T. J. (1975) *A Primer of Psychobiology*. San Francisco: Freeman.

Tharp, R. and Wetzel, R. (1969) *Behaviour Modification in the Natural Environment*. London. Academic Press.

Thomas, A., Chess, S., and Birch, H. (1970) 'The origin of personality', *Scientific American*, August.

Trown, E. A. and Leith, G. (1975) 'Decision rules for teaching strategies in the primary school: personality-treatment interactions', *British Journal of Educational Psychology* 45, 2.

Underwood Report (1955) *Report of the Committee on Maladjusted Children*. London: Her Majesty's Stationery Office.

Valentine, C. W. (1956) *The Normal Child and Some of his Abnormalities*. Harmondsworth: Penguin.

Vernon, P. E. (1975) 'Personality'. In H. J. Eysenck, W. Arnold and R. Meili (eds), *Encyclopedia of Psychology*, vol. 2. London: Collins/Fontana.

Wade, B. (1981) 'Highly anxious pupils in formal and informal classrooms: the relationship between inferred coping strategies and I cognitive attainment, II classroom behaviour', *British Journal of Educational Psychology* 51, 1.

Wankowski, J. (1970) *Personality Dimensions of Students and Some Educational Implications of Eysenck's Theory of Extroversion and Neuroticism*. Birmingham: University of Birmingham Research Report.

Watson, J. B. and Rayner, R. (1919) 'Conditioned emotional reactions', *Journal of Experimental Psychology* 3.

Watts, A. G. (1978) 'Using computers in careers guidance in schools', *Journal of Occupational Psychology* 51, 1.

Weiner, B. (1979) 'A theory of motivation for some classroom experience', *Journal of Educational Psychology* 71.

Wells, B. W. P. (1983) *Body and Personality*. London: Longman.

Wheeler, H. (ed.) (1973) *Beyond the Punitive Society*. London: Wildwood House.

Wheldall, K. and Merrett, F. (1984) *Positive Teaching: the behavioural approach*. London: Allen and Unwin.

White, R. and Lippitt, R. (1960) 'Leader behaviour and member reaction in three social climates'. In D. Cartwright and A. Zander (eds), *Group Dynamics: research and theory*. New York: Harper and Row.

Williams, J. M. (1961) 'Children who break down in foster homes', *Journal of Child Psychology and Psychiatry* 2.

Wiseman, S. and Start, K. B. (1965) 'A follow-up of teachers five years after completing their training', *British Journal of Educational Psychology* 35, 3.

Witkin, H. A. (1959) 'The perception of the upright', *Scientific American*, February.

Witkin, H. A. (1965) 'Psychological differentiation and forms of pathology', *Journal of Abstract Psychology* 70.

Witkin, H. A., Lewis, H., Hertzman, M., Machover, K., Meissner, P., and Wapner, S. (1954) *Personality through Perception*. New York: Harper and Row.

Name Index

Subject Index